WHAT DO YOU DO WHEN ... ?

A Handbook for
Classroom
Discipline Problems
with Practical
and Positive Solutions

Robert L. Gervais
Delos A. Dittburner

UNIVERSITY
PRESS OF
AMERICA

LANHAM • NEW YORK • LONDON

Copyright © 1985 by

University Press of America,® Inc.

4720 Boston Way
Lanham, MD 20706

3 Henrietta Street
London WC2E 8LU England

Library of Congress Cataloging in Publication Data
Gervais, Robert L., 1937-
   What do you do when —?

   1. Classroom management.   2. School children—
Discipline.   I. Dittburner, Delos A., 1936-
II. Title.
LB3013.G47   1985   371.1'024   85-13551
ISBN 0-8191-4810-5 (alk. paper)
ISBN 0-8191-4811-3 (pbk. : alk. paper)

All University Press of America books are produced on acid-free
paper which exceeds the minimum standards set by the National
Historical Publications and Records Commission.

ABOUT THIS BOOK

The data presented in this book were not researched with formal procedures. The authors met once or twice a week for three years and brainstormed through each problem. Problems and solutions were also discussed with fellow administrators and teachers. Therefore, the classroom problems and their practical solutions all stem from the authors' personal experiences as teachers and administrators.

This book addresses specific classroom management problems. Similar problems are grouped into chapters and are approached from the classroom teacher's point of view. Each problem is defined and discussed as to why it is a concern to a classroom teacher. This is followed by an analysis of the various approaches which a teacher can utilize to solve the problem. A summary of solutions is also provided at the end of each section.

The authors believe this text will also be a useful source of information to administrators and counselors when assisting teachers with classroom problems.

The pronoun "he" refers to both male and female and is used only for convenience.

INTRODUCTION

This book deals with classroom management problems and solutions. Problems are discussed from a classroom teacher's point of view. The authors have avoided discussing problems from an administrative, parental or student perspective. This book deals with specific problems and offers specific solutions. This is not a philosophical book. Problems most frequently encountered by teachers are addressed in a practical straightforward manner. A wise teacher will have a method of dealing with a problem rather than floundering when under pressure. In short, the authors believe classroom management must precede teaching.

Classroom management is a method of procedures and behaviors which will eliminate or reduce specific disruptive acts. It is necessary to develop a set of procedures which excludes pure punishment as a method to correct a situation. Effective classroom management is not physically or socially painful, but will reduce the probability of an undesirable response.

The position is taken that most students are basically find young people and respond positively to proper classroom management techniques. Coercion, intimidation and violent acts will not inspire a student to love learning. An orderly classroom does not insure learning, but order does insure that all students will have the opportunity to learn. It is advocated that you establish procedures for most classroom activities. For example, you should have a policy for sharpening pencils, asking questions and collecting assignments. Simple routines minimize confusion and maximize time for students to learn.

The authors feel that the decline in achievement test scores and the increase in the nation's discipline problems are directly related to poor classroom management policies. Many teachers spend an inordinate amount of class time dealing with discipline problems rather than instruction. Effective classroom management gives teachers "time to teach". The authors suggest a possible "back to basics" movement in the area of classroom management. All too often, some teachers find themselves frustrated and exasperated due to their inability to cope with classroom problems.

You will find throughout this book that a middle of the road approach to classroom management is advocated. The most successful approach is somewhere between the teacher as a tyrant (Weatherspoon) and anarchy. It is realized that what works for one teacher will not necessarily work for all teachers. Therefore, several solutions are suggested for each problem. These suggestions are proven techniques employed by highly successful teachers.

Students respond positively to teachers who treat them as worthwhile human beings. If students have healthy self concepts and respect for others, they will refrain from disruptive behavior.

A healthy and positive teacher attitude is also an essential ingredient for successful classroom management. Too often, teachers unwittingly reinforce disruptive behavior through their own negative response to minor classroom incidents. Unfortunately, some classroom discipline problems are in effect created by poor teacher attitude toward students. The authors believe that successful teachers sincerely like and enjoy the students they are teaching.

The authors advocate the use of private student teacher conferences to deal with most classroom discipline problems. Open and public student teacher confrontations are usually not successful. Students generally will resist being embarrassed in front of their peers. This often least to a "no-win" situation. Modern day teachers can no longer expect blind obedience from students. Today's students expect rational explanations and reasons for rules and regulations.

Classroom management problems can also be diminished when the teacher is highly motivated and excited about the learning process. This helps establish a positive classroom climate and further reduces problems.

The authors believe that you will find this book a practical approach to classroom management. Much has been written from a theoretical or philosophical base in the area of discipline. Unfortunately this literature offers few practical solutions for the classroom teacher. Everyone would agree that it is best to anticipate and prepare for problems before they occur. No one should have to say ---- "What do you do when...!!"

TABLE OF CONTENTS

Chapter I
PROBLEMS THAT WASTE TIME

Not Bringing Required Materials to Class

Have you ever forgotten anything? Most people often forget important things. Students are like many adults, and they do forget. Usually students are taken to task for forgetting assignments or special clothing and supplies.

Why should you be concerned about this seemingly minor problem? Consider for a moment what chaos would result if half of the students were unprepared and asked for permission to go to their locker for forgotten items. Little if any order or teaching would take place since teachers would be busy writing passes. Also, too often educators assume that these failures are acts of defiance or designed to irritate. Remember, you are dealing with an age group that by nature is somewhat irresponsible.

One might take the philosophy that unless you are prepared you might as well not be present. Good old Weatherspoon has a simple, straightforward rule: Not prepared - F for the day - three F's for not being prepared and you fail for the grading period. This inflexible rule may work for Weatherspoon but more humane methods are advocated for handling this problem. Hopefully, education and exposure to responsible individuals will help young people mature. Over-forgetfulness can cause problems for adults and can result in loss of job, income and happiness. However, we forgive adults for occasional forgetfulness - possibly students deserve equal treatment.

As a classroom teacher you must be able to anticipate problems and "head them off at the pass." You must have confidence that you can handle classroom management problems. Hopefully, you won't be as unyielding as Weatherspoon. Therefore, you must make classroom rules with which you and your students can live. Insure that students understand your rules. This will make life more pleasant for everyone. Keep accurate records. Make a note of how often Johnny forgets. Chronic forgetfulness requires corrective action such as a one to one conference or a phone call to the parents. Another suggestion is to stand by your door so you can observe your classroom and the hallway. When a student approaches your room without books or other materials, stop the student at the door with instructions to get the required material. The response will probably be, "I'll be late and have to go to the office and will receive a detention." (Or whatever form of punishment is used for being tardy). Stand firm and soon the students will bring necessary supplies with them.

1

Another reason for standing near the hall is that a teacher's presence in the hall reduces pushing and other minor forms of misbehavior. Unruly behavior usually is carried over into the classroom which can make getting the class underway more difficult.

Many schools have a school store which can help alleviate this chronic amnesia. Encourage your students to stop by the school store before school and during class breaks to purchase needed supplies. If your store does not presently offer credit encourage the sponsor to consider establishing a credit policy. Remember, the student who forgets pencils and paper probably has also forgotten money to purchase these supplies.

The most commonly forgotten items are books, paper and pencils. Since many teachers do not wish to have students leave the classroom to retrieve forgotten items, let's examine some procedures which the teacher can utilize within the classroom.

Why not consider keeping extra books on hand and loaning them to students. Do not allow students to take these books out of the room. This can easily be handled by assigning a student the task of checking the number of extra books on hand. Requiring students to sign a notebook is also helpful. If some consistent procedure is not adhered to, the extra books will soon disappear.

What are you going to do when you make an assignment and several students do not have paper? The procedure you follow should be one that causes the least disruption to your planned lesson. A supply of scratch paper is readily available from the school office or where the ditto machine is located. Students should understand that they should quietly obtain a sheet of this scratch paper or borrow from their neighbor.

The "no pencil problem" can be easily handled by having a pencil jar in the classroom. Students without pencils should be instructed to quietly borrow a pencil from the jar or a fellow student. A supply of pencils is readily available on school floors. The custodial staff will usually cooperate by supplying you with pencils they collect while sweeping.

Another proven method is to occasionally conduct a materials check. This is done by somehow rewarding those students who have brought to class all required materials. This reward can be extra points toward a grade. This encourages responsibility and is positive rather than punitive.

Forgetting materials can be an even greater problem in such areas as physical education and vocational classes. Not having cloth in sewing class, or wood in wood shop, and tennis shoes in

Many of our previous suggestions can be helpful but in these cases, a telephone call to the parent is usually in order. You might consider an alternate lesson plan for students who come to class unprepared. For example, a student who has forgotten gym shoes could go to the library and write a paper on the particular activity you are teaching that day.

In the case of chronic offenders, consult with the counselor, nurse, or building administrator. These cases may involve defiance, apathy, or indigent families. Resource people can offer suggestions for handling these special problems. Remember, there may be valid reasons why students come to class unprepared.

Always give a student the chance to redeem himself. You must be flexible, yet not a pushover. If it comes to someone being wrong, let it be you. By being to severe or unbending you may alienate yourself from a student who forgot something for the first time.

Also, by believing students, you'll find they respect you for trusting them. The habitual offender must be corrected but "go easy." Probably the best way to correct this problem is to set a good example and remember that often "children will act like children." If students can learn to become responsible for coming to class prepared to learn and work, it will help them as adults. Employees are expected to bring the tools of their trade with them.

SUMMARY OF SOLUTIONS

1. Make sure your students completely understand what materials they are expected to bring to class each day.

2. Be consistent! Don't vary your requirements from day to day.

3. Recognize the fact that occasional forgetfulness is a common human trait.

4. Reduce the necessity for leaving the room by maintaining a supply of extra materials in the classroom. You might consider establishing a loaner's desk with necessary equipment and make students sit there and leave materials there.

5. Whatever methods you employ, make sure your procedures are designed to reduce distractions and save time for instruction.

6. Allow forgetful students to borrow pencils, paper and share books.

7. Maintain a record keeping system so as to identify those students who chronically forget required materials. Conduct student-teacher conferences with students who abuse your procedures.

8. The responsibility of bringing required materials to class carries over to real life situations. Use examples as to what would happen to their parents, if they repeatedly forgot the necessary materials for their jobs.

9. Stand by your door between classes and stop students who try to enter your class without proper materials. Send them back to their lockers. A few tardies with detention periods may serve as a helpful reminder to bring materials to class.

10. Encourage the use and availability of a school store during passing periods.

11. Conduct a materials check every two or three weeks and award bonus points to students who come to class prepared.

12. Maintain a pencil jar.

13. Students who borrow your extra supplies must return these materials prior to the bell. Require that students write their name on the board and the item borrowed. This will help avoid having materials "walk" out of the classroom.

14. Be on the lookout for indigent students who may not be able to purchase required materials. Refer such cases to a counselor or call the parents.

15. Most adolescents need help getting organized. Advice on organizing material may result in an improved record of arriving prepared.

16. You may wish to require "make-up time" for lost time going back to lockers.

17. Low achievers often function better when most material is left in the classroom.

18. Use the last few minutes of each class period to remind students of required material for tomorrow's class.

19. Not bringing required material to class may be intentional. An occasional locker check will verify if the item is indeed "lost" or "left at home."

Unauthorized Items in the Classroom

Students often bring items to the classroom other than school-related materials. These unnecessary items are disruptive to your classroom and may endanger the well being of students. It is the responsibility of the classroom teacher to prevent the entry of undesirable items into the classroom. What are some of the things which do not belong in the classroom?

Let's first discuss innocent items which probably do not disrupt the learning process nor are they dangerous, but tend to clutter a classroom. Reference is made to items such as combs, coats, hats, scarves, boots and even curling irons. Let your students know early in the school year that you expect these items to be left in their lockers. After all, these items are not related to the learning process.

Other items, much more disruptive than combs, also find their way into the classroom. Items such as balloons, rubber bands, whistles, water pistols, and pornographic materials can greatly disrupt a well-planned lesson. These types of items are attention getting devices and certainly do not belong in a classroom.

The list of and use of items pranksters bring to class goes on and on. Consider the following rules for the items described above. Tell your students that items not related to classroom learning do not belong in the classroom. Pick up combs, radios, lipstick and other unnecessary items. The first time you take an item, the student can pick it up after school. The second time they bring an unauthorized item to class, the student will be required to pick it up from the principal's office. The third time, the parent must come for a conference. By always allowing the return of an item, you cannot be accused of stealing.

There is still another category of unauthorized items which are not only disruptive but also endanger the well-being of students and teachers. These types of things cannot be handled in the suggested manner as outlined above. Examples of unusual and dangerous items are knives, firearms, and even animals. In cases such as these, the item in question and the student involved must be immediately removed from the classroom and referred to an administrator. At this point, the classroom teacher's responsibility ceases.

You may think this is a rather severe procedure; however, you are concerned with more than just the academic achievement of your students. Teachers are or should be concerned with student's social development, their comfort, and certainly their safety.

5

You, the classroom teacher, must be aware of what each student is doing at all times. This is one of the main rules of classroom management. Someone is always in control of every classroom and it might was well be you. If you lost control of even minor areas such as discussed in this section, you may be headed for difficulty. It is much easier to never have relinquished control of the classroom than it is to regain it.

SUMMARY OF SOLUTIONS

1. Stand by your door between classes and carefully observe students entering your room. Be alert for unusual packages or objects.

2. Specify what will be allowed and what will not be allowed in your classroom.

3. Confiscate undesirable items. Return normal items with an admonition to not being them again. Items which may cause serious problems should be turned over to the principal.

4. Make sure students understand your procedures for dealing with undesirable materials in the classroom. Always state that a certain object can be retrieved after class or in the principal's office. This will avoid the connotation of a teacher stealing from a student.

5. Never forget the danger inherent in the multitude of undesirable objects in school.

6. Rule: "If we don't use it in class, don't bring it."

7. Some items may be acceptable in certain classes but not in other classes. Students should be required to place these items in a predetermined place and pick them up after class.

Time Management / Digressions

There is a direct relationship between the amount of time a teacher actually instructs and the level of student achievement. It is suggested that you analyze your instructional periods. How much time do you spend

1. Taking attendance

2. Disciplining students

3. On make-up work

4. Digressions

5. Study periods

6. Actually teaching

Dr. Ethna Reid of the Exemplary Center for Reading Instruction in Salt Lake City, states that often only a few minutes of a class period is actually spent learning. Whether or not you agree with Dr. Reid, many educators feel there is much wasted time in schools. It is possible that non-teaching time is related to the national problem of low achievement scores. It is also possible that the national discipline problem is related to poorly planned and utilized class time. Students tend to become disruptive when they are not involved in a meaningful learning experience.

Digression, or not staying on the subject, is one of the major wasters of time. Teachers and students often do this unintentionally when they begin talking about personal experiences. Sometimes students intentionally initiate digressions to avoid work.

Many students seem to have an uncanny animal-like instinct when it comes to sensing some hard work ahead. They ask the teacher a question about past experiences and then encourage elaboration. When the bell rings the teacher realizes the entire period has been used talking about traveling in Mexico or being on the front lines during the Korean or Viet Nam War. Young people have relatively short attention spans and sometimes it may be desirable to "drift off" the subject. But, if you find yourself doing this too often, you may wish to take corrective action. The critical thing is to know how you spend your class time.

You should be aware that most classes have a power structure. Certain students are capable of wielding considerable influence over the class. This may include asking irrelevant questions as well as other disruptive acts. First, identify the informal student leadership. Then, get the leaders involved in the learning process. The rest of the class will usually follow examples of the acknowledged leadership.

The best way to avoid digressions is to make your classroom policies known to the students early in the year. Tell them that during a learning activity, all questions and comments must pertain to the lesson. If you feel compelled to do so, reserve the last few minutes of each class period for a general discussion of such things as big games, hunting seasons, school contests, and other items of current interest. Most students will respect a fair rule such as this one.

In the final analysis, the best way to effectively manage class time is through planning and organization. Poorly planned lessons result in much wasted time, increased frequency of digressions, and numerous discipline problems.

SUMMARY OF SOLUTIONS

1. Use a stop watch to help you analyze how you use a class period.

2. Identify the power structure in each of your classes then try to direct the leaders' actions in a positive manner.

3. Set aside a few minutes each period to talk about interest-things. This may be used as a reward for cooperation.

4. Consistently enforce a policy of acknowledging only pertinent comments and questions.

5. Digressions can be used as motivational tools or rapport building techniques - if kept in moderation.

6. There is no substitute for a well prepared and organized lesson.

7. In the final analysis, good classroom management procedures are the best way to maximize "time on task."

Writing Notes in Class

Note writing is not one of the more serious problems facing classroom teachers. The question may be asked, what concern is it of the school if students write notes? As with all other problems discussed in this book, student activities become a concern when they affect the learning process.

No one knows how many notes some students write during a school year. However, any custodian will tell you "lots." Try to imagine how much time is spent writing five or six page notes - and oh, how the English teacher works to get a two paragraph theme out of most students. Much valuable class time is wasted; also gossip seems to be spread in this manner.

If notes become a problem in your classroom, Weatherspoon has the answer, read the note aloud in the class. Any student who is embarrassed or humiliated by this action will make sure a note is never again discovered in his possession in your class. Unfortunately, the student may hate you forever.

Along with other classroom rules, explain to your students early in the year that you do not approve of writing personal notes in class. Be sure your students understand the reasons for your rule: wasted time, spreading gossip, and the litter caused by tearing up notes to destroy them.

What course of action will you take if note writing becomes a problem in your classroom? Plan ahead and have a prepared procedure. Many teachers simply pick up notes and keep them until the end of the period or school year. An even better procedure is to tell the student to come in and pick up the note after school. This will provide the opportunity for a student-teacher conference regarding the problem. However, be careful about publicly demanding a note. Because of the highly confidential nature of notes, a student may refuse. Confrontations of this type are usually no win situations and they should be avoided. The section on defiance suggests several ways of dealing with this type of open challenge.

When you do pick up notes it is a good idea to be alert for potential problems. Some students literally pour their hearts out in these notes. Look for indications of serious problems, such as: drugs, runaways, suicide, pregnancy, fights, or just malicious gossip. Problems of this magnitude should immediately be referred to the building principal or counselors. Conduct yourself in a professional manner; do not make the mistake of discussing personal notes with others unless it benefits students.

Well planned and organized lessons and activities will prevent excessive note writing. Moving around and being cognizant of all student activity is still one of the best ways to prevent problems.

SUMMARY OF SOLUTIONS

1. Move around the room and be aware of what each student is doing at all times.

2. Discuss the negative aspects of writing notes with your students and let them know you expect positive and constructive efforts in your classroom.

3. Explain your procedures - that all notes are to be put away or they will be picked up and may be re-claimed during an after school conference.

4. Tell your students that you are not interested in the personal gossip contained in notes.

5. If a student becomes an habitual offender, turn the notes over to principals, counselors or parents.

6. Avoid acts of defiance by not "grabbing" or demanding that notes be given to you. Simply ask that they be put away and not used in your class.

7. Reading student notes can destroy your rapport with students. Notes are often of a very personal nature.

8. Never read notes outloud in class.

The Classroom Wanderer

Every class seems to have at least one wanderer. That is a student who can't seem to stay put. These students always need to sharpen a pencil, borrow something, throw paper in the waste basket or get a book from the shelf. The list of needs seems to go on forever.

You might ask why you should be concerned because a student needs to move around to satisfy his needs. Usually the wanderer disrupts at a crucial point, such as, when you're giving directions or somebody is giving an oral report, thereby interferring with the learning process. Another reason for concern is that "wandering" while the teacher or another student is talking is considered very poor manners.

This problem is easily overcome by simply not allowing it. Early in the year explain that such acts are not only disruptive but are discourteous. If you take time to explain the rule and why it is needed, you will find that most students respond in a positive manner. As with any classroom rule, be prepared to make occasional exceptions. In this case, students should have the right to quietly take care of emergency needs.

Don't confuse the wanderer with a hyperactive student. (See section on hyperactivity). Also, a devious student may use this technique, along with a polite "I forgot" to disrupt your class. This may be another gimmick to gain attention. Occasionally you'll meet a student who truly doesn't understand or forgets. Insure that you go the extra mile, and then some, for these students.

To prevent excessive wandering during study periods try the age old honor system. That is, allow one boy and one girl out of their seat at a time. If this procedure is violated - cancel the privilege for the rest of the period. Peer pressure often insures that students stay in their seats.

While giving directions, what will you do if a student gets out of his seat? Stop talking immediately and stare at the student until he is back in his seat. Another technique is to just quietly say, "I'll see you after class."

Keep a record of these minor incidents as suggested in other sections. Do not be too punitive with students who infrequently violate this rule. Take more serious action for the habitual or chronic offender.

11

SUMMARY OF SOLUTIONS

1. Accept the fact that a certain amount of movement around the room is a necessary and integral part of the learning process.

2. Accept the fact that adolescents can't sit still as long as adults.

3. Organize class movement so that certain times are designated for sharpening pencils, cleaning up, or picking up supplies. This will concentrate disruptions and decrease noise during lessons and study periods.

4. Make sure students understand that you disapprove of unnecessary wandering and the effect it has on the class.

5. Use record keeping systems to identify the chronic abusers and follow up with conferences.

6. Refer students to counselors if you suspect physical hyperactivity.

7. Seat hyperactive students close to supplies, wastebaskets and pencil sharpeners. This will decrease disruptions caused by their movement.

8. Pick up worksheets, tests, and other material in order to keep students in their seats.

9. Plan your classroom management procedures so as to eliminate most reasons for student movement during class.

Telling Lies, Fibs and Excuses

There is a natural human tendency for self protection and survival. Many people have found that they can avoid punitive action for the commission of undesirable acts through fabrications and distortions of the truth, or telling outright lies. These habits are formulated in early childhood and often continue through school years and into adult life.

A wise teacher will be aware of these facts and expect similar behavior from some students. The problem is like a double edged sword. You will have problems if you never trust or believe your students, and you will also have problems if you always believe them. You must learn how to cope with this dilemma.

Please consider the following dialogue which frequently occurs in classrooms:

Teacher: "Where's your homework?"
Student: "My dog ate it!"

Teacher: "Where's your progress report?"
Student: "My mother washed it!"

Teacher: "Who wrote on this desk?"
Student: "I didn't!"

How would you handle these situations?

Usually these confrontations take place in front of the class. Your behavior is almost forcing the student to lie to "save face" or avoid punishment. It might be better to simply say, "Let's discuss this after class privately."

Avoid impulsive reactions to student excuses. You should quietly and consistently check out or investigate these stories in a professional manner. This entails using discretion in some instances and yet being very open about your investigation in other cases. In effect, what you have done, is protect the student from embarrassment. Yet, students should know that you will not accept everything on face value. You can avoid problems by simply requiring all excuses to be written and signed by the responsible parties such as parents, teachers, or coaches.

Another problem is exemplified by the following dialogue: "My children lie? Never!" This is often stated by parents and teachers who should know better. This is another example of why proof is very important. About the time you angrily call a parent about little Johnny always lying, rest assured that the

13

mother will state, "Well, yes, the progress report did go through the washer. I meant to call you today."

Another neat trick of some students is to completely change the story when sent to the office. Make sure you have thoroughly communicated your position orally or in writing to the principal.

Keep in mind that a teacher's responsibilities go beyond the instruction of subject matter. You are also expected to teach such concepts as morality, responsibility, and indeed - honesty. Foremost, be honest and fair yourself. Reward truthfulness whenever possible.

SUMMARY OF SOLUTIONS

1. Be aware of the fact that a certain percent of communications received from students will be fabrications and distortions of the truth.

2. Humanistic treatment of students will decrease the necessity to lie out of fear of punishment.

3. A procedure which contains checks and double checks will help prevent lies, fibs, and excuses.

4. Open confrontations encourage lies.

5. As a general rule, require written excuses from parents. A consistent policy will avoid a feeling of personal stigma.

6. Never accuse without positive proof and then do so privately.

7. Reward truthfulness whenever possible.

8. Create an organizational scheme which reduces the necessity to make excuses or lie.

9. A parent conference with the student present will often solve most problems.

10. Make a list of the common situations when students lie or make excuses. Analyze your problem areas and devise procedures which will eliminate or reduce the necessity for lies and excuses.

Chapter II
TEACHER PREPARATION

Lack of Proper Planning

The problems caused by lack of proper planning can be illustrated through some realistic situations which unfortunately too often take place in classrooms. Consider the following:

1. It is Monday morning and you haven't read over the new chapter, run off new worksheets or checked the calendar. In short, you didn't prepare any lesson plans.

2. You are suddenly called out of town because of family illness. You do not have a written plan for the week and your grade book and seating charts are at home.

3. The afternoon assembly program has been cancelled and your classes will meet after all.

4. Everyone completed the test and over half of the period is still left.

5. The films did not arrive in time for Friday's classes.

6. The principal is visiting class today and wants to see your long and short range goals and objectives. He also wants to see your grade book, lesson plan book, seating chart and attendance records.

These situations often lead to teacher panic, student pandemonium, and a lack of learning. Students will act up and not work when they are placed in a situation with inadequate leadership. Planning and preparation do not always result in success but they certainly increase the odds.

A statement frequently made by some teachers is, "Those kids were terrible today." This often happens due to weather changes and the excitement associated with anticipation of school activities such as dances and games. However, it is also possible that the poor behavior was the result of poor teacher planning. Remember, planning is also anticipation. Wise teachers will think through their lesson plans and anticipate problems.

It is also possible students were acting up due to a boring or uninspiring lesson. Meaningful learning is the best prevention of discipline problems in the classroom. Try to avoid excessive use of dry old lectures and open book reading. Be creative and prepare lessons which utilize educational games, role playing, discussion groups, contests, simulations, case studies, and community involvement. Whenever possible, your

15

lessons should be interesting, student centered, and varied so as to promote a high degree of student interest and involvement.

It is also important to have alternate plans (emergency plans) to take care of unexpected interruptions such as epidemics, weather, and substitute teachers. You should also anticipate and check on schedule events such as assemblies, field trips, parties, guest speakers, and other activities which influence your daily routine.

Most teachers have a favorite lesson or two such as an educational game, activity, or contest which students thoroughly enjoy. These should be placed in your plan book and saved for that day when everything seems to fall apart.

Another critical area of teacher planning is to anticipate the necessary materials required by your lesson and to have them ready and available. A lack of materials such as glue, rulers, or graph paper can ruin what may have been a good lesson.

It is also important that you consider the problems and questions that students will have regarding your lesson. This is especially true when planning activities such as labs or group activities. Your directions should be thought out carefully and given clearly to ensure a minimum of interruptions.

Time management is another aspect of proper planning. It is your task to teach several periods each day. Poor planning can waste time and therefore decrease student learning. There is a positive correlation between utilization of class time and achievement scores. This requires avoiding unnecessary digressions and adherence to a planned time table.

SUMMARY OF SOLUTIONS

1. Well planned, organized, and interesting lessons prevent discipline problems.

2. Develop alternate lesson plans for emergencies.

3. Good teaching is the result of hard work by a teacher.

4. Anticipate questions and problems associated with your lesson. It will save time and avoid confusion.

5. A team approach to planning will result in new ideas and stimulation to organize and prepare for lessons.

6. Plan a variety of activities for each class period.

7. Update your lesson plans after each class and each day. Don't place yourself in the position of having to ask specific classes what has been covered.

8. Identify desired learning outcomes prior to starting a new unit.

Preparing for Group Activities

Classes can be conducted in a variety of ways. A typical class may be a sequence of lecture, discussion, and study period. In all three cases, teacher and students are acting as a unit and doing the same things at the same time. Often these methods also invoke strict policies such as:

1. One person at a time talks

2. Students stay in their seats

3. No unnecessary movement of materials or equipment

In other words, the class is teacher centered with all activity revolving around the teacher.

Group activities are defined as two or more students working together as an independent entity. For clarification, the following are examples of group activities:

1. Two students orally drilling each other on spelling words

2. Three chemistry students preparing an experiment

3. Five students working on an oral presentation

4. Several students being tutored by the teacher

5. Several groups working on worksheets in a competitive manner

Even though group activities may be good teaching methods, they offer the potential of more classroom management problems than the teacher centered approach.

The very nature of group activities results in students talking, moving around the room, and the transfer of equipment and supplies. This can lead to very noisy situations which may disrupt other classrooms and evolve into utter chaos in your own classroom. This in turn leads to damage and destruction of equipment and supplies. If things get too far out of hand, student safety may become a factor. In all cases, poorly managed group activities result in little or no student learning and a deterioration of teacher authority and respect.

Weatherspoon never has problems with group activities because he never changes methods and always conducts class with oral reading. No one speaks, leaves their desk, or thinks during the entire period. Students may "die of boredom" but no no will be injured or bother the class next door.

As stated previously the authors advocate utilizing a variety of teaching techniques and believe that group activities can be highly beneficial if properly managed.

However, you must realize that worthwhile group activities don't just happen. They are the result of much planning and preparation. In fact, group activities always require more teacher planning than do teacher centered approaches. It is recommended that you consider the following steps when preparing for group activities.

Step one:
Give clear directions as to what you are going to do, why you are doing it, and how it is to be done. Take plenty of time before starting to ensure that everyone fully understands the assignment.

Step two:
Develop special classroom rules and procedures for group work. For example, always make your own group assignments. Select one individual in each group to serve as leader and that individual will enforce the group rules. Allow only one person per group to speak at a time. Everyone must participate and stay on task. Make sure someone is responsible for the final report or summary of work completed.

Step three:
Make sure that all needed supplies and equipment are available in the room. Then, think through the best method of distributing materials to each group. You should assign one person in each group to distribute and pick up needed materials.

Step four:
Think about the time required to give directions, distribute materials, perform tasks, and clean up before the end of the period.

Step five:
Enforce your rules and procedures vigorously because group activities can easily get out of hand.

Motivational Techniques

The subject of students not working is covered in another section of this book. Reasons for not working are many; however, the authors believe the subject of student motivation is so important that it deserves a special section in this text.

Teachers across the country are constantly faced with the dilemma of either having "turned on" or "turned off" students. Obviously, teachers want students to be "turned on" because they will learn more and cause fewer discipline problems. However, there are many obstacles which prevent teachers from achieving this goal. It is impossible to wave a magic wand and suddenly fill the room with excitement for learning. Let's examine some of the problems which must be overcome.

Your personal attitude toward your subject and students may be the single most important factor in determining the degree of success which you achieve in motivating students. A negative attitude will dampen student enthusiasm toward you and your subject. On the other hand, if you sincerely like students and are excited about teaching, your inspiration will transfer to the entire class.

You must also consider the age group of your students. Younger children are more interested in pleasing adults than older students. Secondary students are also interested in school but their reasons may be different. For example, adolescents develop interests in sex, peers, clothes, social events, cars and dances. This complicates the matter of motivation for secondary teachers. It is imperative that you thoroughly understand the age group of your students. This will allow you to relate your teaching to the needs and interest of your students.

Teachers must also be cognizant of the fact that interests in specific subjects vary among individuals. You majored in the subject you teach because this subject was exciting. However, your particular class is only part of a student's school day. Each student studies five or six different subjects and has interests outside of school. Therefore, you can't expect all students to be as excited about the subject as you are. This does not mean that you should not attempt to motivate everyone, but it does mean you should take a realistic approach.

Another problem is competition with outside of school activities and interests. Modern day teachers must constantly compete with television, movies, discos, recreational activities, and jobs. It is difficult for the average teacher to conduct class in as an exciting manner as many TV shows. However, it does point out the fact that today's teacher must be able and willing to use theatrics and drama in the classroom.

20

As pointed out elsewhere in this text, your room environment is an important factor in determining student attitude. In the authors' opinions, some secondary school classrooms are rather drab. That is, there is a general lack of attractive bulletin boards and displays. In fact, too often, these rooms are dirty and cluttered with various supplementary teacher materials and equipment. Imagine the students' reaction to organization and neatness while working in these surroundings.

Many instructors who teach required courses complain that students are apathetic because they are forced into these specific classes. These teachers feel it is easier to motivate students in elective classes due to the fact that students chose to be there. Teachers who feel this way take the chance of transferring this attitude to their students and thereby compounding their perceived problem. As stated previously, you must believe in and be excited about your subject and/or grade level, if you hope to motivate students. A defeatist attitude toward teaching required subjects is totally unacceptable, because the authors have visited too many required classes, where students were excited and enthused.

Parental attitude toward school is another problem that confronts teachers when attempting to motivate students. Parents who have had poor educational experiences often pass on negative attitudes to their children. This may explain a student's reaction to a particular subject or teacher. When this type of attitude first becomes apparent, the teacher should contact the parents and arrange for a conference. Frankly discuss the problem with the parents, solicit their support, and explain that the student's problem may be compounded if this attitude persists. Parents should never criticize the school, other teachers, or subjects in the presence of their child. Parents should not ignore school problems but be encouraged to direct concerns to administrators, teachers, and counselors.

Adequate equipment and supplies are also a factor in student motivation. Teaching materials alone will not create an exciting class. However, if instructional materials are utilized effectively, students may look forward to your class. The authors realize that there is a direct relationship between local financial resources and the availability of supplies. In cases where items are in short supply teachers need to use their ingenuity in terms of borrowing, sharing, and obtaining needed materials. Every community has untapped resources available for educational use such as parents, business, governmental units, and trade groups. These individuals are usually very cooperative when asked for assistance. These groups will also provide guest speakers who may bring expensive and sophisticated equipment which has high student interest.

Inadequate teacher planning is another reason why students are often uninterested in a particular class. Students do not respond positively to teachers who display signs of disorganization. There is no substitute in time spent planning.

Other motivational techniques which you may wish to consider are:

1. Ensure that each student achieves some degree of success. Constant failure causes students to develop lackadaisical or hostile attitudes toward school.

2. Give positive reinforcement throughout your lesson. Students need praise and rewards for their efforts.

3. Do something to excite or create student interest at the beginning of each class. This may take the form of demonstrations, stimulating questions, or references to current events.

4. Vary your teaching techniques. Do not use any one technique such as lecture throughout a period. Use at least three different activities each period such as audiovisuals, discussions, contests, group, or individual work.

5. Establish rapport with students. (See section on rapport)

6. Don't be afraid to use drama in the classroom. Anything that arouses interest in your subject should be utilized.

7. Involve your students in devising interesting learning activities. Students usually respond positively to peer ideas and suggestions.

8. Do you understand the age group that you teach and what "turns them on"?

9. Show excitement and enthusiasm for your subject matter. If the teacher isn't motivated, neither will the students be motivated.

10. Don't be devious about test questions. Be open and straight forward as to what is expected of students.

11. Don't be afraid to use happy grams, positive progress reports, and positive phone calls to parents. Most students will respond in a positive manner.

Teachers must accept the responsibility of motivating students. It is no longer acceptable or productive to blame students for their own lack of interest in school. It is your professional obligation to constantly search for new and effective instructional techniques which will motivate your students to learn.

Go to bed thinking - "How can I turn those kids on tomorrow?"

Planning for the Days before Vacations

Most teachers look forward to well deserved vacations; however, they generally dread the days leading up to vacations. Any experienced teacher knows that they will have to deal with many different problems on these "last days". For example, many students become extremely excitable in anticipation of forthcoming vacations. Their attention span and interest in school is limited; this may cause disturbances and excessive noise. In short, a teacher is competing with highly motivational activities such as a Christmas party, a fishing trip, or numerous other vacation activities.

A vacation usually represents the first "break" students and teachers have had for some time. This may mean that patience is in short supply and tempers are quick to flare. As a result, these tense times can result in very serious discipline problems.

Another problem is students leaving early for vacations. This results in abnormally high absenteeism on the day before a vacation. Because of the absenteeism, many teachers feel it is futile to continue with the normal academic program. The reaction actually compounds the problem. If parents and students feel very little instruction takes place before a vacation, they in turn feel little obligation to attend school. As you can see, those left in school will find disruptive ways to amuse themselves. It appears to be a vicious cycle.

Teachers are also subjected to still another pressure --- class parties. This is especially true in the lower grades before holidays such as Halloween, Christmas, and Valentine Day. Teachers are caught in a dilemma. If you have a party, learning stops. If you don't have a party you're considered an ogre by your students. As you can see, you are in a no-win situation.

So what will you do? No matter when a vacation is scheduled, there must be a last day and it is something which which you must contend. Being aware of the problems listed above is a major step in coping with that "last day". The anticipation of potential problems should motivate everyone to be extremely well prepared no matter what you decide to do. It is strongly advocated that you continue teaching.

Check with your building administrator to make sure that your plans are in compliance with school policy. For example, some schools do not allow parties while others may encourage a relaxed atmosphere.

Continue instruction by utilizing high interest activities, such as educational games or contests. You can also divide up your class period with serious work followed by some lighter but well controlled activities.

Whatever you decide, take adequate time to plan every detail and anticipate the reactions of your class. You might even consider letting your students have a voice in deciding what to do. Students generally respond in a responsible and positive manner when involved in the decision making process.

SUMMARY OF SOLUTIONS

1. It will help suppress student excitement regarding forthcoming vacations if teachers will maintain a rather nonchalant attitude and carry on with "business as usual."

2. Be especially well prepared and organized before vacations.

3. Utilize motivational lessons, which are educational yet maintain student interest.

4. Whatever you do, remember the old axiom: "Keep them busy until the last bell rings."

5. If you must have a party, schedule it for the last 30-40 minutes of the day.

6. Hand out yearbooks the day before the last day of school. Allow students to spend part of each class period signing yearbooks.

When
you've exhausted
all possibilities,
remember this;
YOU HAVEN'T

Dr. Robert H. Schuller

Chapter III
MISSING CLASS

Student Absenteeism

Unless you've been there you will never believe the extra paper work that absenteeism can cause classroom teachers. Depending upon the school, absenteeism can vary between five and twenty-five percent of the student body. Mondays and Fridays often receive special attention for staying home.

Basically, you will have to contend with three types of absenteeism. They are excused absences, truancy, or official suspension from school. Regardless of the reason for being absent, most teachers feel that students should have the opportunity and responsibility to make up missed work. Whatever the reason, this means only one thing for you - more work.

Unfortunately, some parents will allow a student to stay home for almost any reason. Excuses range from helping at home to shopping trips, vacations, severe weather, or just being too lazy to get up and go to school. However, most absences are for legitimate purposes such as sickness or family obligations. School activities also contribute to the absentee problem. This is especially true in senior high schools when students travel out of town for athletic events, debates, and musical performances.

So how are you going to deal with this problem? Weatherspoon and other sour teachers take off X number of points for every day missed for whatever reason. This may work for you, but if you've read this far you're looking for more positive solutions.

If your school doesn't have an established policy for make-up work, you might consider allowing two days for every day missed. This accomplishes several objectives:

1. It is fair and consistent for all students

2. It teaches responsibility

3. It prevents undue procrastination

To relieve you of considerable paperwork, you might consider the buddy system. When one member of the team is absent the other ensures that notes, assignments, and other information are relayed to the buddy. It might be wise for the teacher to keep this information and give it to the absent student when returning to school.

27

An assignment sheet may also work for you. All assignments are written on a large assignment sheet. It then becomes the student's responsibility to read this sheet for all days absent. Naturally, the sheet must be accessible to students.

Some teachers write missed assignments on the back of the admit slip, while others require students to meet with them after school. Another idea is to require a notebook to be kept up to date. Lecture notes, assignments, and other important information are kept in this notebook. Surprise notebook checks can be held and all up-to-date notebooks gain some points or credit for the student. This system helps insure that students bring books, paper, and other materials to class. These suggestions are effective but take up much of your valuable time.

A time saving technique which also improves classroom climate is the monthly calendar bulletin board. This bulletin board can be attractive and yet be large enough to record each day's assignment. Students returning to school after an absence need only to consult the bulletin board. As an additional time saving device, you may consider asking a trusted student aide to keep the calendar up to date.

Selective "class cutting" can also be a serious problem. Older and more worldly students know which teachers do not take accurate attendance or consistently check admit slips. This can make everyone's job more difficult. Remember, you are the only one who can verify if a student was present in your room.

When a student's absenteeism becomes a problem, consider a private conference with the student. Express a real concern. A call to the parents may be helpful. Don't condemn the student or parents but try to determine the reason for excessive absenteeism. By expressing concern you'll not only be a better human being and teacher, but the school and your image will be enhanced.

SUMMARY OF SOLUTIONS

1.   Establish a buddy system for obtaining assignments.

2.   Utilize student aides to assist with taking attendance, keeping records, and checking excuses.

3.   Display assignments on wall calendars, chalkboard, or folders so students returning from an absence can obtain their own assignments.

4.   Post regular office hours before and after school so students can obtain assistance with make-up work.

5. Require all assignments to be recorded in the student's notebook.

6. Be cognizant of the fact that absenteeism is also a part of adult life. Most student absenteeism is legitimate and deserving of positive consideration.

7. Reward students for good attendance by giving extra credit points. However, never lower grades for excused absences.

8. Show concern. When a student returns from an absence let him know you sincerely missed him.

9. Update your lesson plans on a daily and period by period basis. Allow absent students to look at your lesson plans when they return.

10. Prepare a make-up folder for each class period. Put extra copies of all handouts, worksheets, tests, and assignments.

11. Bell assignments will get students to work immediately and allow you time to work on attendance.

12. Individualize assignments for students with extended absences. If every teacher required all make-up assignments from a student who had been out for two or three weeks, the student would be in a most difficult position. Such frustration may lead to more absences.

13. Whatever procedure you choose - don't waste the time of the entire class for one or two absent students.

14. As with most suggestions, these classroom management procedures work only if students are well versed in your expectations.

Being Late

Why should you be concerned about tardiness? Normally, teachers give group directions at the beginning of class. In walks the wayward student and states, "Sorry I'm late, what are we doing?" Needless to say, everyone in class has their attention riveted on this situation. You have a choice. You can either repeat the directions, wasting the time of the entire class, or ignore the late individual and go on with the lesson. Neither situation is good. Students are in school to learn, not waste time.

The "tardy problem" should not be ignored. If you do condone this problem you're really telling students that it's all right to be late, it's OK to waste other people's time, and irresponsible action is approved.

Have you given much thought as to what you're going to do when students are tardy? The authors' experience indicates that around half of all students will be reported to the principal for being late once during the year. It is assumed that many teachers don't send students to the office for the first offense, so it may be safe to assume that virtually all of the student body will be tardy at least once. What action should you, the classroom teacher, take?

Weatherspoon has the answer; it's simple and easily understood. If you're tardy, for whatever reason, you flunk for the day. This might work, but students and parents may rise up in revolt against such arbitrary and inhumane rules.

You should establish a policy whereby every student is expected to be in his seat when the bell rings. When a student arrives late, get him seated and continue with the class. Tell the student that you expect to see him after school. At that time ask why he was late. There may be a legitimate reason. Explain that it is important to be on time to avoid disruption of class. Students should also understand that most employers will not tolerate chronic lateness. Do not take punitive action for the first offense. Normally this is all the action that is necessary. Before you become too punitive, think about the times you've been late!

Do not become overly concerned about the student who is occasionally late. Students who are chronically late do merit your concern and time.

The only way you can objectively differentiate between an occasional and a chronic problem is to keep accurate records. There are several simple and painless ways to accomplish this feat. Consider one or all of the following methods:

30

1. Have students sign a tardy book with their name, date, time, and reason

2. Enlist the help of a student aide to keep records

3. Make a notation in your gradebook or on your seating chart

In all cases, late students should be required to remain after class and explain the reason for being tardy. The teacher will then determine if any punishment will be administered. Punishment may take any of the following forms.

1. Report to the teacher after school for makeup time

2. Refer to the office

3. Call parents

The most positive way to handle this problem is to help students organize their time. The most common reasons for tardiness are excessive trips to lockers, restroom stops, and talking to friends between classes. Several locker trips can be eliminated if students will carry supplies for more than one class. This will allow more time for restroom stops and socialization. Hopefully, this will also reduce the number of times a student is late.

Discussion has been limited to tardiness between classes in a secondary school. The authors feel that being late in the morning or after lunch is an administrative problem and should be handled by the building principal.

SUMMARY OF SOLUTIONS

1. Realize that nearly everyone is occasionally late for something - think of faculty meetings.

2. Don't concern yourself with the student who is late one or twice a year.

3. Don't allow tardy students to disrupt class. They should enter quietly and take a seat.

4. Develop a record keeping system (a sign-in sheet or notebook) to aid you in identifying chronic cases.

5. Instruct students on how to organize their time between class or before school.

6. Don't ignore tardiness or students will develop a lackadaisical attitude toward arriving on time to your class.

7. There are many reasons for being late. Listen to them before administering punishment.

8. Place a "tardy desk" near the door to your classroom. Tardy students are required to sit there until you have time to deal with the problem.

9. Teachers should be at their door between classes helping to move loitering students toward their class.

10. "Three minute bell assignments" which are graded encourage students to be on time.

11. There is usually a reason for chronic tardiness. Enlist help of guidance and administrative personnel.

There seems to be an infinite number of reasons why students ask to leave the room. Many of these requests are valid and necessary. Therefore, you cannot make and hold to an arbitrary rule. You are forced to decide each request on its own merits. Consider the ramifications of refusing to grant a bathroom pass that is desperately needed!

Regardless of the reason, students leaving the room cause many problems for classroom teachers. First, the request to leave probably interrupts your prepared lesson. You must stop whatever you are doing, discuss the reason for the request, then decide whether to let the student leave. This is a waste of teacher and class time, and the student may cause a disruption by bumping a desk or slamming a door.

While in the hall students may make disrupting noises which affect other classrooms as well as your own. Remember, halls and restrooms are usually poorly supervised during class periods. Therefore, the chance for vandalism and other mischievous acts are increased.

When the student finally returns to class you are greeted with additional entry noise and the question, "What did I miss" or "What are we doing?"

You may overcome this problem by using Weatherspoon's philosophy ---- No one leaves regardless of the reason. However, you are already aware of the potential consequences of such an arbitrary rule.

One alternative is to establish a humane policy which allows students to occasionally leave the room and yet prevents abuse and minimizes the disruption to your classroom. This can be accomplished by requiring students to sign a notebook and record the date, time, and destination.

This procedure allows students to leave the room when necessary, is not disruptive, and gives you a record. You may wish to have student/teacher or parent/teacher conferences regarding students who appear to be abusing the privilege. Experience shows that most students shy away from signing such a notebook unless it is absolutely necessary. You should also be able to use some type of permanent hall pass with a sign-out system. This further reduces the disturbance and waste of time involved in writing passes.

A good general rule is never deny a request to use the bathroom. Also, do not publicly question the need for the request. It's rather embarrassing for all concerned when a student loudly states why it is necessary to go to the bathroom. The authors know of two recent cases where junior high students actually wet their pants in class. The maturation of adolescent girls adds to this problem. Can you imagine how difficult it would be to handle the embarrassment to the student and then explain to the parents why permission to use the bathroom was denied.

If you find that your "Bathroom Charlie" is taking advantage of you, refer him to the school nurse. If this doesn't cure the problem, suggest a conference involving the student, nurse, parents, and yourself. Seldom, if ever, will it go this far.

Let students know they have the right to use the bathroom. Also, insure that your students know they may leave the room anytime they feel ill. Just tell them to fly! If and when this happens, send another student to check on them to insure they are all right.

Be cognizant of the fact that no matter what you do, some students will have to leave your room during class time. Anticipate problems and be prepared to deal with them in an orderly manner.

If you don't, you'll find that everybody "has to go" in your room!

SUMMARY OF SOLUTIONS

1. Devise a painless record keeping system of who leaves the room and the reason for leaving. Require students to sign a notebook with date, time and reason.

2. Check your records for possible abuse and conduct private student/teacher conferences with those who appear to be abusing your procedures.

3. Discuss your procedures for leaving the room thoroughly with all students so they understand and will keep distractions to a minimum.

4. Encourage students to check with you prior to the bell if a trip to the restroom or nurse may result in being late to class.

5. Check with your building administrator prior to using permanent passes.

6. Require students to make up all time spent out of the classroom either before or after school. This allows a

student to make a personal decision, but should deter unnecessary trips.

7. Check your sign-out sheets with other teachers to see if certain students are abusing "hall passes" in all classes. Refer chronic cases to your building administrator.

8. Students who appear to be abusing the "restroom pass" may be required to go to the nurse and use the bathroom facilities in her office.

9. Establish a portable water cooler in your room to cut down on requests for a drink in hot weather.

10. Cut down on requests for leaving the room by keeping an extra supply of items commonly left in lockers.

Teacher Absenteeism

Teacher absenteeism falls into three basic categories:

1. Unanticipated personal illness or problems which occur prior to the beginning of the school day.

2. Anticipated absenteeism for such things as professional meetings, school activities, or personal business.

3. Unanticipated emergencies or illness which occur during the school day.

Regardless of the reason for absenteeism, problems may crop up simply because the regular teacher is not present. In nearly all cases, there is a reduction in student learning. No matter how you approach this problem, it is very difficult to maintain continuity of instruction.

The problem is further compounded depending upon the type, quality, and qualifications of substitute teachers available in your geographic area. Substitute certification requirements vary from state to state. The overall competence of your substitute will be directly proportional to the problems created by your absence. In many cases, these problems are compounded due to the unavailability of substitute teachers. Classes may have to be combined or sent to a study hall.

Discipline problems generally increase in number and severity when the regular classroom teacher is absent. This is primarily due to two things:

1. Many students have what appears to be an innate drive to test and torment a substitute teacher.

2. Substitute teachers are at a disadvantage because they do not know the students, classroom rules, school policies, or instructional program.

All of the above problems directly affect the absent teacher. When you return, you may also be confronted with the loss of materials and equipment due to thievery or vandalism. The fact that your class was out of control during your absence caused not only physical damage but resulted in a lack of instruction. You are now faced with going back over the lessons which should have been covered during your absence. Regaining control of the class may also be a problem.

Subject matter areas such as vocational education, music, band, and physical education pose unique and different problems. Not only is it more difficult to obtain qualified substitute teachers in these areas, but student safety and the possibility of damage to expensive and specialized equipment affects the well being of the entire school.

Weatherspoon is not concerned with these problems. Weatherspoon comes to work even when sick, never attends professional meetings, and would never think of getting involved in student activities. In other words, Weatherspoon feels indispensable and is always there to spread negativism.

Unlike Weatherspoon, you must recognize the fact that occasional absences from work are unavoidable. Therefore, you must take certain steps which will minimize the problems previously discussed. Anticipate this eventuality and begin to prepare yourself and your students.

Consistently prepare clear, concise and written lesson plans. These plans, along with seating charts, grade book, classroom rules and procedures, school policies, and specialized substitute instructions, should be left in your room and readily accessible to a substitute teacher.

Appoint one or more students to assist the substitute. These students can be most helpful with such things as taking attendance, explaining procedures, and locating materials and equipment. Your seating charts should indicate which students can and will help in these matters.

Develop specialized lesson plans over subject matter with high student interest. This will solve the problem of continuity and allow the sub to initiate an activity or lesson which the students will enjoy and react to in a positive manner. This will create a learning experience for your students, while decreasing the probability of classroom management problems.

Make sure students understand your expectations when you are absent. Explain the difficulties that a substitute teacher encounters. Most students will respond positively when they understand the scope of the problems.

Your substitute plans should make it very clear that you expect teaching and not "babysitting" when absent. Students should understand your attitude and also that the sub will summarize student achievement and behavior. You must hold your students accountable for their actions during your absence

The authors have observed that substitute teacher problems vary from room to room. The only common variable seems to be the attitudes and classroom management techniques of the regular classroom teacher. Substitute teachers who work in the rooms of teachers who consistently employ sound classroom procedures have significantly fewer problems. Obviously, good classroom management techniques carry over to days when you are absent.

SUMMARY OF SOLUTIONS

1. Anticipate that you will occasionally miss school and prepare your students and lesson plans for such an eventuality.

2. Update all lesson plans at the end of each school day.

3. Maintain a special drawer or file with all pertinent forms, gradebook, schedules, seating charts, attendance records and anything else a substitute teacher will need. Make sure the administrator is aware of the location of these materials.

4. Devise a special high interest lesson plan, with all necessary materials, which a substitute could use during your absence for a period of one to five days.

5. Call your substitute whenever possible.

6. Appoint a student helper in each class to assist substitute teachers.

7. Talk to students about the problems of being a substitute teacher. Appeal for cooperation rather than agitation.

8. Require that your substitute complete a daily log of all activities including disciplinary problems. Follow up on these activities when you return and deal severely with troublesome students.

9. Your attitude toward substitute teachers will carry over to your students.

10. Request specific substitutes whom you know and trust. They will probably do a better job than a complete stranger.

11. Don't come to work sick.

Chapter IV
TALKING IN THE CLASSROOM

Excessive Talking in the Classroom

Talking itself is not a problem. It becomes a problem when it distracts from the learning process. Consider the following situations where talking is a problem in the classroom.

1. When it interrupts others

2. When it prevents listening

3. When school announcements are being given

4. When a teacher is giving directions

5. When a student is reciting or giving an oral report

6. When you have a guest speaker

7. When showing a film

8. When trying to change from a talking to a non-talking activity

9. When it requires repetition

10. When one person dominates classtime

11. When talking is not on the subject

12. When a teacher talks loudly to one student during a work period or test

13. When students talk during a test

Too much talking and too little listening seem to be a plague of modern society. Talking out of turn and disrupting the class is rude, and just another example of poor manners. Also, if allowed to go unchecked, this talking may be a prelude to more unruly behavior which may result in the classroom teacher eventually losing control.

How then, you might ask, can this far reaching problem be handled? Weatherspoon has a simple solution ---- Weatherspoon does all the talking. To avoid the Weatherspoon approach, you must be extremely well prepared and organized. This will eliminate many classroom problems, but specific recommendations follow.

It is imperative that you learn to read the mood of the class. You must be able to understand students. If a controversial issue is bothering students, take time to bring it out in the open. You may not solve the problem but offering a forum may satisfy the class. Some form of recognition must be developed when large group instruction is taking place. The old standby of raising hands for recognition is not without merit.

What if a student interrupts you while you're talking to the class? One method is to simply stop talking and stare the student down. Never, and we mean never, try to out talk or out shout a student in the classroom.

You might keep the violator after school for a private conference. Explain to the student how his behavior is disrupting the class and solicit cooperation. If conduct grades are given, develop a record keeping system of each outburst. One way of doing this is called the "dot system". The dot system can be implemented by recording dots on the seating chart or grade book. Five dots and you call home, express your concern, and ask for parental help. Ten dots and it's a trip to the office. Fifteen dots and the conduct grade is "F".

Other things to keep in mind are:

1. On the first day of school explain to the class that one person at a time will talk unless involved in laboratory or group activities.

2. Explain the purpose of the tardy bell ---- this should mean quiet. It should not be necessary for a teacher to tell a class to quiet down after the bell.

3. Physically separate the talkers by changing their assigned seats.

4. A teacher should set an example of good listening habits by not interrupting a student who has permission to talk.

A word of caution here, you must enforce your rules. Just think how many times some teachers or parents warn children but never do anything. You must decide how many times you'll warn and then carry out your end of the bargain. Hopefully, by mixing your classroom activities you'll avoid excessive teacher talking and students will "tune-in" rather then "tune-out", which is all too often the case.

SUMMARY OF SOLUTIONS

1. Establish classroom rules for talking during the first few days of school and consistently enforce your procedures. (Require raised hands with teacher recognition prior to talking.)

2. Allow students to discuss critical issues and let off "a little steam" prior to indulging in quiet work.

3. Never try to talk over and above student talking.

4. Never give instructions until everyone is quiet and looking at you. Blink lights or ring a bell for attention.

5. Conduct private conferences with students who interrupt class by talking.

6. Develop a record keeping system for disruptive acts such as names on board, a notebook, dots on seating chart, or have a student aide assist you.

7. Change your entire seating chart several times or until you have the best arrangement to reduce unnecessary talking.

8. Explain to your students that interruptions by talking are considered poor manners in adult society.

9. Ask students to apologize for interruptions.

10. Call on students rather than "raise hands". This will also enhance listening.

11. Call on students who are talking without permission.

12. Avoid talking at the end of assignments or tests by having the next activity ready and organized.

13. Stare at offenders until they quiet down.

14. Stand in close proximity to offenders.

15. The teacher should always stop talking immediately when a student interrupts. Do not continue until you have everyone's attention.

16. Use mild sarcasm (carefully) like "We are waiting for Charlie's attention."

17. Learn to ignore minor talking as when a student borrows paper or pencil from a fellow student.

18. Examine your questioning techniques.
    a. Do your questions solicit shouting out answers by many students?
    b. Are your questions directed to a specific student?
    c. Do you always call on specific individuals?

19. Use listening devices such as:
    a. "We'll have a short quiz at the end of the period."
    b. Some questions on tomorrow's quiz are....
    c. Ask Tom to repeat your directions.
    d. Ask Jim to repeat what Jean just said.

20. Require students to record their own offenses of talking out of turn.

21. How good are you, the teacher, at giving directions? Thorough directions prevent the necessity of student questions and in general unnecessary talking. Do you get your students working then interrupt them for further instructions?

22. Your "oral reprimands" interrupt everyone. When necessary, "oral reprimands" should never exceed five or ten seconds. A large number of "oral reprimands" may be indicative of a poorly managed classroom.

23. Substitute non-verbal cues for oral cues whenever possible.

24. Reward students with a few minutes of quiet "chit-chat" at the end of each period for being cooperative.

The Blurter

Mr. Joe Blurter is quite different from the student who just enjoys talking or irritating you. Often this person is a good student who enjoys school. The problem is that he gets excited and just blurts out comments.

It's great having "turned on" students in class, but usually this person interrupts right in the middle of something important. He just can't control himself. A student of this type can easily dominate class discussion. As a teacher, your goal should be to involve as many different students in the discussion as possible. The blurter prevents this or at least makes attainment of this goal very difficult.

Blurting can also become contagious and spread to other students. Soon, your orderly classroom will be in pandemonium. At this point you feel like resorting to Weatherspoon's solution ---- tape their mouths shut.

Start the school year with the age-old method of requiring students to raise their hands when they wish to speak. Explain to your students why this policy is necessary. Your reasons may include the following:

1. Interrupting others is a display of poor manners

2. It is difficult to hear if several people talk at the same time

3. A few people will dominate all class activity and exclude the shy or quiet students

4. Blurting will lead to a disorderly classroom

Most students will respond in a positive manner when you have taken time to explain classroom rules.

The individual student who continually violates this rule should be kept after class for a student teacher conference. If the problem is not corrected, you may wish to refer the problem to parents, principal or the guidance department. Keep in mind that many of these students do not understand why their actions are inappropriate.

In serious cases, you may wish to consider some type of behavior modification techniques. An example of this would be to require the student to daily record his own "blurts" and turn it in at the end of the period.

43

If all else fails, you may have to remove "Mr. Blurt" from the classroom. Isolation is often a very effective disciplinary technique with outgoing students.

Recognize that every classroom will have an occasional "blurt". You will have to use your discretion as to when this becomes a problem and action is required.

SUMMARY OF SOLUTIONS

1. Insist that students always raise their hands and be recognized prior to talking.

2. Set up a system where the teacher always calls upon students - no one raises their hands.

3. Require "blurters" to keep a record of their interruptions. Use these records in student teacher conferences.

4. Use isolation techniques for severe cases such as the back of the room, hall, or office.

5. Be consistent - don't allow interruptions one day and punish the next.

6. Explain to students that interruptions such as "blurting" are disruptive, poor manners, and infringe on the rights of other students.

7. Use non-verbal cues such as "thumbs up" or "thumbs down".

8. Ignore students with minor or infrequent blurts. Do not recognize their comments or answers until called upon.

Swearing, Obscene or Profane Language

Certain types of language or words are offensive to various people. Obscene words, gestures, and literature, when used in the classroom, can cause embarrassment, disruption of the learning process, and the teacher to lose control of the class. Therefore, you must determine what limits will be allowed in your classroom.

This is more easily said than done, since certain words which are in common usage in particular areas or homes may be very offensive to individuals from other walks of life. Remember, your class is a melting pot of the entire community. It is made up of various social classes, races, nationalities, religions, and value systems. Your job, as a teacher, is to instruct all students without alienating any particular group.

At the beginning of the year, tell your students that obscene words, gestures or literature will not be tolerated. When you announce this rule, like all others, explain why you think it is important. The authors will almost guarantee you'll have some students who will state, "But everyone uses those words." Some students will even ask, "What words do you mean?" Don't fall into the trap of listing these words on the board. Virtually all students are familiar with the most common "dirty words" in vogue at the time.

The authors realize there are many borderline words. When these are used, simply state, "That word is not used in this classroom," and go on with the lesson. Student challenges may be a problem. They may state that their parents use a certain word. It is suggested that you emphasize these rules and apply them only to your classroom and that you do not dictate behavior in other places. It would be wise to follow up such challenges with a private student teacher conference. Insure that you do not belittle the values of students and parents. Students often report that other teachers allow or use profanity in their classrooms. Thank the students but do not make a public statement. This delicate problem must be handled in an appropriate manner. You should consider a private conference with the building administrator.

Now that you have a rule against swearing, what will you do if a student breaks this rule? If it is a slip, talk to the student privately. If it continues, call home or have a conference with the parents. If the problem still persists, send the student to the office. In cases where profanity is directed at you or another student, send the student to the office immediately.

Another aspect of this problem is pornographic literature. Students often bring commercial or original writings and pictures to class. Confiscate such items and give them to the principal or the student's parents.

It seems many students and adults feel it is cute or popular to swear. Individuals who normally wouldn't use such words will do so because of peer pressure. Don't bend and buckle, just stick to your rule ---- no foul language in this class. Remember, exemplary behavior and speech on your part will go a long ways in alleviating this problem.

SUMMARY OF SOLUTIONS

1. Explain to your students at the beginning of the school year that you will not tolerate name calling, swearing, or slang language.

2. Never ignore a swear word. Take some type of action such as writing the student's name on the board or keeping the student after class.

3. Teachers must set an example by never using swear words and minimizing the use of slang words and nicknames.

4. Profanity which is directed at the teacher should result in an immediate referral to the principal.

5. Watch out for words with a "double meaning".

6. Don't ask the student what he said as this gives him the opportunity to change the word or deny it.

7. Tell students that certain words offend you personally even if they don't seem to offend others.

8. Teach students to adapt to different situations since the acceptance of certain words may vary.

9. Teach students acceptable vocabulary which can easily replace profane words. This can be a humorous way to expand vocabulary and simultaneously reduce swearing.

10. Don't allow students to wear clothing with "sayings" or "words" that would not be allowed orally.

11. If you refer a student to the office for swearing, require the student to write the word on the misconduct referral form.

12. In most cases, a very firm "We do not use that word in this classroom" may suffice. Do not argue. You make the rules in your classroom.

Beginning is
half the
battle

Chapter V
TEACHER CREATED PROBLEMS

Accurate Records Versus Generalizing

Teachers often make comments such as "Johnny is always talking," "Suzie never brings materials," or "Sam is forever coming to class late." Comments such as these are usually made by frustrated teachers in lounges, at parent conferences, or to students in classrooms. These statements are almost always generalizations and exaggerations devoid of any factual basis. They do nothing to help alleviate the problems. Conversely, unprofessional and inaccurate statements such as these tend to provoke a student's sense of fair play. It certainly is not a good method to improve rapport with students and gain respect of parents. In fact, teachers often find themselves unable to defend statements during parent or administrator conferences as a direct result of such generalizations.

What a teacher needs is some simple facts! Unless, of course the teacher happens to be Weatherspoon. Weatherspoon punishes all offenders regardless of circumstances. Most educators disagree with Weatherspoon and admit that anyone can make an occasional mistake like forgetting or being late. Your concern should be directed toward those students who habitually cause disruption of the learning process.

You should be concerned with factual data. Exactly how many times did a student actually commit an undesirable act in your classroom? This is behavioral analysis and must precede behavior modification. You must have accurate date to identify problems before you can correct them.

"But..." teachers will say, "I don't have time to keep elaborate records; I'm already too busy." You must be convinced that good record keeping is very important and not an impossible task. How will you do it?

Your first step is the same as described in other chapters. Make a list of classroom rules and the type of information needed. You may want to consider such things as: interruptions by talking, making excessive noise, tardies, trips to the locker or bathroom, and any other offenses which would normally be handled by you.

Your second step is to ensure that all students thoroughly understand that you do not expect abuse of your classroom rules. Emphasize that you can understand occasional errors but will not tolerate excessive abuse of any rule. In fact, not only will you not tolerate abuse, but you intend to record all acts of misconduct. Let your students know that, if necessary, you will

49

provide the principal or their parents with dates and numbers of all infractions. In other words, your conduct grades will be as objective and factual as your academic grades.

One simple system is to let your students do the record keeping for you. Reserve a blackboard, bulletin board, or clip board for this purpose. Establish a routine whereby each student must record his own act of misbehavior. Example: students arriving late for class must sign their names and time of arrival. The same procedure is used for other offenses such as forgetting supplies, going to the bathroom, or locker. If you have had to warn a student for some minor misbehavior you can direct him to record the incident. You may prefer to record such information yourself, or assign a student aide this task. Either way, recording the data must be a quiet and well established routine which does not interrupt normal classroom activities: It will only take you or your aide a few minutes at the end of each day to record the information on some sort of chart or record sheet.

Your data will enable you to make sound decisions based on factual information prior to referring students to the counselor or administrator, or calling a parent. Conduct grades will now be more objective and accurate. Students respect the accuracy and fairness of this system and will soon realize that they are accountable for conduct as well as academic grades. If this system is handled in a humane and professional manner, soon there will be few incidents to record. Students generally react positively to an organized and well managed system. It will no longer be necessary to exaggerate and generalize.

SUMMARY OF SOLUTIONS

1. You must accept the premise that conduct records require objective and conclusive date.

2. You must also accept the fact that conduct records can be maintained without expending a great deal of time.

3. Require students to record all misconduct in a classroom discipline notebook.

4. Mark your gradebook or seating chart in code to indicate discipline infractions.

5. Assign a given number of conduct points to all students at the beginning of each grading period. Each infraction of class rules results in a loss of some of those points. The total remaining points at the end of the grading period determines the conduct grade.

6. Use your records to convince students and parents of the problems. Follow-up these conferences by implementing individual contracts designed to diminish or eliminate the problems.

7. Student aides can be utilized to record discipline problems.

8. Finally, records may save the day if you ever have to go to court regarding a student discipline problem.

Too Many Students Gathered Around the Teacher

Where is the teacher? What is that mob of students in the front of the room? Upon closer examination you find that in the middle of that mass of humanity, there really is a teacher's desk and a teacher. Serious problems can arise out of situations like this.

Why should you be concerned? First, it is impossible to see what is happening in the rest of the room when surrounded by students. Also, when you're having a discussion with your favorite students, the less outgoing students who really need help can't get your attention. In fact, you may alienate a large percentage of the class who feel and actually are ignored. You may open yourself to charges of being overly friendly with students. (See section on over-friendliness with students)

You may also find that items disappear from your desk. Past experience indicates that valuable personal items as well as answer sheets, gradebooks, teacher editions, and tests are regularly reported stolen or lost. Adequate supervision prevents occurrences of these types. It is simply not possible to provide good supervision and individual student help with a large group of students around your desk.

Weatherspoon doesn't have this problem. You can probably guess why. Students are not allowed to leave their seats or ask questions. Unfortunately, Weatherspoon also never leaves his desk or offers individual student help.

A far more effective technique is for you to move around the room. Help not only those who ask for help but check the work of everyone.

If you must sit at your desk during a study or work period, only one student at a time should confer with you, with no line. The desk should be located at the back of the room. This should be explained the first few days of school along with all your other rules.

In fact you should closely examine your use of study periods. Do they meet the objective of your lesson? Is each student utilizing this time wisely? And finally, is this the best way to use your time? Study periods with individual teacher help are effective only if well planned and organized. Obviously, with a large group of students around you, it will be very difficult to meet the above criteria.

SUMMARY OF SOLUTIONS

1. Establish a classroom rule early in the year that no more than one or two students may be at your desk at any one time.

2. Get in the habit of helping students at their desks.

3. Sitting behind a desk is a poor supervisory technique. It encourages writing on desks, note writing, doing other than required work, and various other negative behaviors such as cheating.

4. This problem will never occur if you constantly move around the room.

Overfriendliness With Students

As stated in the chapter on rapport, the authors advocate a positive student teacher relationship to foster communication and learning. However, if this relationship becomes too "buddy-buddy", serious problems can arise. Unfortunately, adolescents have difficulty in differentiating between student teacher relations and their own peer associations. If allowed to go unchecked, a student will often push a teacher's attempts at rapport into an unpleasant situation which causes a teacher to lose the respect of many students.

Students have a problem in knowing when to stop, how far to go and in general don't know how to handle these situations. The kidding and joking goes on and on. Suddenly the teacher finds that to show the class he means business he must display complete and total anger and students don't understand.

Most teachers want to be liked and respected by students. However, the old but true statement that familiarity breeds contempt still prevails. This can result in losing your authority and leadership role in the classroom. At this point, loss of control can be such that very little learning will take place.

Weatherspoon never has this problem, since he is never pleasant to anyone. It is not suggested that you follow this example. There are steps you can take which will allow you to be a pleasant, friendly person yet will keep you from becoming overly involved with your students.

You might consider using proper names at all times. Insist that students always refer to you as Ms., Mrs., or Mr. On the other hand, never use potentially embarrassing student nick names unless requested to do so by a student or parent. This will help ensure your not getting overly involved in the personal lives of students. This is not to say you cannot be a good listener and act as a problem solver. It will, however, help you to maintain your professional image. Stress politeness and good manners at all times. This helps prevent over-familiarity and also develops habits of thoughtfulness and consideration in your students. A thoughtful teacher will not joke with individual students. Joking with the entire class will prevent individual embarrassment and ridicule. If you tell slightly off color jokes to students they will assume the right to reciprocate and this can soon get out of hand. Remember, teachers are employed to educate children, not win popularity contests.

Teachers who feel they must treat students as peers often do so out of insecurity or lack of confidence. If you are a bit insecure, compensate for these feelings by being very well prepared with interesting lessons.

Overfriendliness with students may also cause you to lose the respect of your colleagues. Many educators resent teachers who act unprofessional. The majority of students don't want teachers to conduct themselves in a childlike manner and resent those who do. The same applies to teachers who try to use student slang.

Research indicates that students work harder and learn more when in the class of a teacher which they like. It is a fine line between a friendly and an overly friendly teacher. It's your task to determine where this line should be drawn.

SUMMARY OF SOLUTIONS

1. Insist on formal titles such as Mr., Mrs., and Ms. This establishes a polite, yet professional distance between teacher and student.

2. Always refer to students by their proper names. Avoid the use of nicknames.

3. Do not discuss your personal problems with students.

4. Do your best to be businesslike and formal, yet also be friendly, courteous, and polite. Remember, you want respect and rapport, not a friendship.

5. Good teachers and classroom managers gain the lifetime admiration of their students. Teachers who strive for instant popularity gain very little enduring respect.

6. Do not engage in the telling of suggestive jokes.

7. Do not associate with students on a social basis outside of school.

8. Remember that your students are not your peers.

9. Be very careful to treat all students in a similar manner. If not, you will be accused of showing favoritism and will lose rapport and respect of students.

Teacher Errors

It has often been stated that "to be human is to error". This may be more true of teachers than other segments of society. The very nature of teaching requires you to constantly answer questions, present information, and make decisions in public. This compounds the opportunity for error.

The following is a list of common errors made by teachers:

Misspelled words	Incorrect grades
Mispronounced words	Covering up an error
Giving wrong answers	Punishing wrong student
Unsafe working conditions	Attendance
Use of profanity	Overly severe punishment
Controversial issues	Loss of temper
Demonstrations that don't work	Threats

An error is a problem within itself, but it becomes more serious when teachers attempt to "cover up" or refuse to admit the possibility that they made an error. Actions such as this can lead to loss of rapport and respect of students. Even worse, errors made in the area of safety can result in serious injury to students. Errors such as these may be construed as negligent acts which can lead to legal problems.

Weatherspoon doesn't have problems such as these. Anyone who dares ask a question that he is not sure of is told, "Don't ask stupid questions - stupid!" or "You look up the answer, dummy!" In other words, he never admits he is wrong.

Teachers should be completely honest at all times. If an error occurs admit it to your class. In fact, it's a good idea to explain your philosophy of "teacher errors" to your class early in the year. Simply tell your pupils that you are only human and will occasionally make errors.

Errors can also become a learning experience. For example, tell your students if they ask a question you can't answer both of us will have a homework assignment -- look up the answer. Start the next day's class with a discussion of this item.

Adequate planning and preparation will eliminate most teacher errors. This is especially important in the area of student safety. Be sure you are complying with all state and federal safety laws.

Teachers are academically well prepared and the errors discussed in this section rarely occur. However, you should anticipate the possibility of teacher errors and be prepared to deal with them in a professional manner.

SUMMARY OF SOLUTIONS

1. Tell your students at the beginning of the year that you probably will occasionally make an error.

2. Thank students for reminding you of your errors and freely admit to them. Never chastise a student for such a correction.

3. Develop questions and errors into homework assignments for both students and teachers.

4. Thorough planning and preparation will eliminate most errors.

5. Don't try a "snow-job" or "cover-up".

6. Don't get angry and blame students.

7. Ask students to look up answers to questions and report back to the class tomorrow.

The Physical Setting

Much has been written in recent years stressing the importance of a positive school climate. The physical setting of a classroom is an integral part of the total school climate. The authors believe there is a relationship between the physical setting of your classroom and the productivity of students. Your task as a classroom teacher is to provide the best possible learning environment. This may not have been critical years ago, but today's students expect a comfortable and attractive place to work.

The physical setting of a classroom becomes a problem to you as a classroom teacher when it has a negative effect on the learning situation. Can you imagine how the following students remarks would affect your classroom.

1. My desk is broken or squeeky

2. It's too cold; or it's too hot

3. My table is dusty

4. Will you turn the lights on or off

5. Can we open or shut the window

6. There's mud under my desk

7. The drapes don't work

8. The window won't open

9. Why don't you have nice bulletin boards

10. I smell something

All of these items relate to the comfort of students. Because students expect certain classroom conditions, you will be forced to interrupt your lesson and handle problems as they arise.

The physical setting of your classroom can also affect the attitudes of students. A bright, well-decorated room may be inspiring and motivate students. Many people work and think best in orderly, clean, and attractive surroundings.

Take time to organize your room so that everything is kept in a consistent, neat, and orderly manner. Such neatness and order adds to the positive climate of the school while also providing efficient management. Disarray is a great time waster and leads to general confusion. You should work closely with your custodian and principal to ensure that classroom equipment is operating correctly and in good repair.

Add to the attractiveness of your room by providing colorful and relevant bulletin boards and wall displays. Witty cartoons, student projects, and current events add to the general appearance while improving the learning environment. Student committees can be responsible for different physical aspects of your room. They can organize books, chairs, workbooks, pull the drapes, put up displays and bulletin boards. This gives your students a sense of belonging and will save you time for instructional purposes.

Change your seating chart and the position of your desk several times a year. Everyone enjoys an occasional change of scenery. When possible, allow students a voice in this decision. Again, it helps to establish a democratic atmosphere which in turn enhances learning.

Encourage students to bring interesting show and tell items if they relate to your lessons. Flowers and plants grow well in many rooms and are appreciated by nearly everyone. They can also become a learning experience as you observe their changes.

A true scholar may be able to study and learn in a dingy cellar; however, most students are in need of stimulation and motivation. Your professional obligation is to do everything possible that will encourage learning. Yes, this may include a little tidying up and dusting.

SUMMARY OF SOLUTIONS

1. A neat and well organized room is motivational and a time saver.

2. Maintain your classroom by immediately reporting items which need repair or replacement.

3. Involve your students in all aspects of room environment. This ranges from putting up bulletin boards to picking up before the bell.

4. Your attitude toward room environment will carry over to your students.

5. Change the physical arrangement of your room several times during the school year.

6. Accept the fact that the physical setting of your room is important and is your personal responsibility.

Never

let a problem

become an excuse

for not taking charge

of your classroom.

Chapter VI
GETTING ALONG

Knowing Your Students

Good teachers really care about their students; they realize that a student is more than a name. Good teachers also take time to get to know their students. Knowing your students means having knowledge of such things as:

1. Physical disabilities

2. Ability and achievement levels

3. Social and psychological differences

4. Interests

5. Family environment

Some educators disagree with the opening statement. They believe that prior knowledge about students affects teacher expectations and therefore student achievement. The authors believe it is most unprofessional to allow such information to negatively affect a teacher's attitude. By not knowing pertinent information, students can be embarrassed or, even worse, psychologically and academically impaired. This may lead to severe discipline problems in the classroom.

Consider the true case of a new teacher who has having difficulties with a boy named Teddy. One day Teddy would work and behave like a "champ". The next day Teddy would do nothing and knocked over desks on his way into or out of the classroom. The problem went on for some time until another teacher asked, "How's Teddy doing this year?" The inexperienced teacher poured out the whole story. The other teacher said, "Well you know Teddy has muscular dystrophy and often can't control himself." Our young teacher was shocked and embarrassed by his lack of knowledge of the physical disability of this student. If your school issues a list of students with physical or mental disabilities - study it - know your students. If such a list isn't published, find out why.

Be alert for abnormal or deviate behavior. Sudden change may be a signal that something is wrong. Another true story is about the boy who was involved in a fatal accident and for some reason started behaving in a very disruptive manner. After spending a couple of days at home he was back to his old self. A variety of things can upset students, such as divorce, child abuse, illness, death in the family, or drug abuse.

Another problem concerns academic disabilities. Consider the embarrassment and psychological impact of asking a non-reader to read orally before the class. This same disability is often the cause of student failure since he can't read your test questions or written work.

Parental attitudes and values vary from school to school. There are also differences in religious, ethnic, and occupational background. These affect parental attitudes and beliefs toward school, which in turn determine student behavior and learning styles. The wise teacher will avoid many problems by being informed about the community in which he works. Good sources of information are: autobiographies, listening to students, cumulative files, permanent record cards, school nurses, counselors, other teachers, sponsors or coaches, administrators, and don't forget the school secretaries. Be sure to handle this type of information in a professional manner. Do not allow it to deteriorate to a form of gossip.

As you can see, there is a lot more to a student than a name. However, even a name can cause a teacher problems. Not knowing a student's name or mispronouncing a name may alienate that particular individual.

Do not emulate our friend Weatherspoon. He considers subject matter of paramount importance. Human needs are never considered.

SUMMARY OF SOLUTIONS

1. You will know a great deal about your students by the end of the school year. You can gain this information accidentally or intentionally. The authors urge you to do so intentionally.

2. Knowing your students is the first step in developing rapport.

3. Knowing your students will help to avoid embarrassing situations.

4. Utilize permanent records which contain information about the physical, social and academic status of your students. These records are usually kept in the main office, nurse's or guidance office.

5. Autobiographies and personal interest inventories are other ways to learn about students.

6. Be aware of school activities in which your students participate.

7. Knowledge of students should be kept confidential unless divulging this information will benefit the student.

8. Private student/teacher conferences will enable you to better know your students.

9. Use questionnaires to identify the "learning styles" of your students.

10. Students have "behavioral styles". Knowing each of your student's "behavioral styles" will help classroom management.

Establishing Rapport or Classroom climate

Just what is rapport? Most dictionaries define rapport as harmonious accord or a relationship which makes communication possible. The authors suggest that teaching and communication are synonymous. It is difficult to find an effective teacher who does not communicate well with students.

Lack of student-teacher rapport can result in many problems in the classroom. For example, research and experience indicates that successful teachers make a strong effort at building good, positive relationships with students. Students learn more if motivated by a teacher they like and respect.

In a recent study, teachers and students expressed concern regarding their mutual relationship. Teachers said many students were not courteous and were disrespectful. Meanwhile, students stated that some teachers were constantly "putting us down" or "belittling us". It is essential that teachers establish a positive classroom climate as early in the year as possible.

Another reason for being concerned with classroom rapport is as a society we have become conscious of the importance of human relations. Labor statistics show that more jobs are lost due to poor human relations than for any other reason. We can no longer run a class like Weatherspoon, who usually says, "Sit down, shut up, and get to work."

An important ingredient in establishing a good classroom climate is your attitude toward young people. Before you sign that first contract or renew your present one look in the mirror and honestly answer the following questions:

1. Do I like young people?

2. Do I get along with the age group I am going to teach?

3. Do I believe in my subject?

If you can't answer with a strong, enthusiastic "yes" to these three questions, consider taking employment in a field where you need not deal with students.

For those of you who answered in the positive the following suggestions are offered for your consideration. Be positive and respect your students. You will come to trust them and they will trust and respect you. With trust and respect comes friendship. If you have these three ingredients you'll have a most rewarding experience as an educator.

Please do not misconstrue this discussion on rapport as advocating the establishment of a "buddy-buddy" relationship with students. (See section on overfriendliness with students.) You must be self confident and not expect problems. If you are hesitant and expect difficulties, be prepared for the self fulfilling prophecy. A positive attitude on your part will prevent most problems and go a long way in establishing rapport.

Remember, students can sense when you are trying to "fake it" or pretend you like them when you really don't They know when you are really happy to be there working with them.

Specific steps which you can take to establish a positive climate are:

1. Know your subject

2. Approach classes with a serious purpose

3. Conduct class in a business like and efficient manner

4. Plan thorough and exciting lessons

5. Set reasonable, clearly understood rules and then fairly administer them

6. Respect yourself and your role

7. Respect students - be polite and courteous

8. Treat students as individuals

9. Deal with issues

10. Don't embarrass individuals

11. Do not show favoritism

12. Ensure you give praise to all students

13. Reprimand in private

Learn the names of students as soon as possible. Use your seating chart and call students by name. Better yet, get a copy of last year's student annual and study names and faces so you know your students as soon as possible. Show an interest in your students and what they feel is important. Much information of this type can be obtained that first day of school by using some form of introduction technique. One that works well for one of the authors is used as follows:

1. Have students put the following information on a large card:
   a) Name
   b) Something interesting about self
   c) Any other information you want

2. Let students mill (walk) around looking at cards

3. Select someone they don't know or don't know well and talk to them.

4. Introduce their new acquaintance

5. Collect the cards and you'll have some information for your files

6. Take a few minutes at the beginning of each class to use this data. For example, ask individual students how they fared in the activities in which they have expressed an interest.

7. Make an effort to personally attend school and community functions in which your students are involved.

You might also consider conducting a class meeting. Allow students to debate the merits of classroom rules. This leads to better understanding, vents feelings and emotions, and improves rapport and socialization. Teachers should spend most of the time listening and directing discussion. Don't argue or get defensive. Don't answer for the principal - in fact, invite the principal to one of your meetings. Remember, everyone, including students, appreciates the opportunity to have input into decisions which affect them.

Another reason for being concerned with classroom climate is a very selfish one. Experience indicates that the risk of violence decreases when teachers establish positive relationships with students. You probably do not have to be reminded of the large number of teachers assaulted by students in recent years.

As a teacher you must expect your rules to be tested. This is normal student behavior. However, if you have established good rapport your problems will be minimized. For example, oftentimes you will need only to exhibit or show disappointment to a student who has violated your trust. In such cases, this can be the most severe discipline that could be administered.

SUMMARY OF SOLUTIONS

1. Be positive and respectful toward your students.

2. Do not use sarcasm, nicknames, or anything that may be construed as a putdown.

3. Display a sincere interest in school activities in which your students are involved. The same applies to outside of school interests.

4. Students generally respect teachers who are well prepared with stimulating and organized lessons.

5. Never openly embarrass students and always reprimand in private.

6. Always take time to explain why you have certain rules or assignments.

7. Compliment students whenever possible.

8. Let students have some input in planning class activities.

9. Be honest at all times.

10. Attend school activities whenever possible.

11. Don't belittle youth culture, fads, and interests.

12. Eat lunch with students.

13. Don't "preach".

14. Show enthusiasm! Studies show that master teachers are enthusiastic teachers.

Fear of Calling Parents

One of the most effective classroom management techniques is obtaining parental cooperation and support. Experience shows that most classroom problems can be diminished or eliminated when parents and teachers work together. However, far too many teachers exhibit a reluctance to call or contact parents. Why?

Calls from school traditionally carry a negative connotation and no one enjoys delivering bad news. Also, some teachers still adhere to the fallacy that they must handle all problems without assistance or be considered incompetent.

Consider calling parents early in the school year before serious problems develop. This initial contact will establish a working relationship which will hopefully assist in solving future problems. It is helpful if this initial contact is of a positive nature. Keep in mind that many parents feel uncomfortable talking to teachers for a variety of reasons. Do not misconstrue parental anxiety as an indication that they do not wish to cooperate.

When you call parents, pay careful attention to the following items:

1. Check names - parents and students may not have the same last name. Mrs. Clark does not want to be called Mrs. Jones and have to explain. Check student records in order to be as knowledgeable as possible.

2. Identify yourself - "This is Miss X from school - I'm Johnny's teacher."

3. State that there is no emergency. Ask if it is convenient to talk now. This is doubly important if you're calling the parent at work.

4. Tell the parent that you need their assistance with a problem regarding their child.

5. Explain the nature of the problem but do not be too critical or defensive. Tell the parent, "I'm concerned about Johnny because...."

6. Try to determine the parent's attitude.

7. If the parent wants to talk - then you should listen. Don't interrupt and agree where possible. This is especially important if the parent is defensive or hostile.

8. Ask the parent for suggestions and don't push the conversation.

9. Don't generalize! Stick to factual statements and the issue under discussion. Don't philosophize or discuss situations that you are not familiar with.

10. Never call when you are angry or upset.

11. Try to come to an agreement on a cooperative action to remedy the problem.

12. Don't make commitments or promises that you can't deliver.

13. Agree on some form of follow-up to the conversation even it it's a "no news will be good news" statement.

14. Mention the positive aspects of the child in question and thank the parent for their support and cooperation.

Remember, the student is important to the parent and a part of American folklore is that a good education is important for success. We honestly feel that if you call parents as a concerned person you'll get their help and support. This will make your job much easier.

SUMMARY OF SOLUTIONS

1. Please note that most solutions are summarized in the steps outlined above.

2. Set a goal of calling two parents each week to report positive accomplishments.

3. Teachers have a professional obligation to keep parents informed - especially when it concerns poor progress academically or as a citizen.

4. Never forget that communication with parents is a valuable tool in maintaining good classroom management.

Parent Conferences

Parent conferences are in many ways similar to telephone calls (see previous section, Fear of Calling Parents). However, they differ in many aspects due to the physical proximity of the teacher and parent. Phone conferences are generally easier to conduct in that you need not be concerned with physical surroundings, personal appearance, or eye contact. On the other hand, people sometimes become more belligerent on the telephone while a personal conference seems to have a mellowing effect on both parties. Another difference is that personal conferences generally reflect more serious problems than telephone conferences.

You might ask, how and why do teachers get involved in parent conferences? The most common reasons are grades and discipline. The request for a conference can be initiated by either party. This request usually follows a negative incident in school such as failing grades, teacher punishment, or for that matter as a result of any of the problems discussed in this text. Occasionally, conferences are called by a third party such as an administrator, counselor, or social worker.

In most schools, parents can call the school office and the secretary will arrange a conference during the teacher's planning or preparation time. It is helpful if secretaries will determine the reason for this request and inform the teacher. This will allow you to properly prepare for the conference.

Now that a time has been established, where will you meet? Many conferences end up being held in the school office, hall or in front of a class. It is strongly suggested these conferences always be conducted in private, such as an empty office or classroom. It is also helpful if the conference room is comfortable and attractive. As stated elsewhere in this text, physical surroundings can affect the attitudes of all involved.

Weatherspoon never worries about parent conferences. This teacher always conducts conferences in a most hostile environment. Parents feel threatened due to the many negative remarks made about their child and perhaps the manner in which they have raised their children.

It is hoped you will always enter into your conferences with a positive attitude. Never do anything to make a parent feel threatened; don't be defensive; don't down-grade the student and family and above all make sure the parent understands your genuine concern for their child.

It is also critical that you properly prepare for each individual conference. Know your subject well - which in this case is the student in question. Get your data together and preview your goals for the conference - you must be confident, and being prepared helps assure your confidence.

In the conference - be specific, don't talk in generalizations. Show the parent the student's work, your record of discipline incidents, and give parents suggestions on how to help their child.

Keep in mind during conferences that parents are forming an opinion of you and possibly the entire school This may be the only source of information a parent has about you and the school other than their child. The manner in which you conduct a conference, your personal appearance and your attitude and knowledge will determine whether you have gained a supporter or an enemy. Your career as a teacher is much easier if you work with cooperative and supportive parents.

SUMMARY OF SOLUTIONS

1. Don't be defensive and listen.

2. The majority of parents are very cooperative and helpful.

3. Be sure you find something good to say - not all negative comments.

4. Check records of grades, ability and general information in cumulative folders before your conference.

5. Give parents a chance to give suggestions for solutions to the problem.

6. Encourage parents to talk, listen to them. Try to determine their attitude toward school and their child.

7. Face-to-face conferences are more positive than telephone conversations. People are more reasonable.

8. During a conference, try to see the parent's viewpoint as well as your's and the school's.

9. Send a progress report home as a follow-up to the conference in two or three weeks.

10. Be sure you have a positive, confident attitude and express a desire to help the student. Don't argue. It will only increase resentment and resistance.

11. Ask parents for help, get them on your side.

12. Be sure to begin and end a conference on a positive note. Thank the parents for coming to see you.

13. Invite a principal to sit in on a conference which you think may be negative, or when the parent is angry and upset with you and the school.

14. Get information about parent's names and work schedules before calling or setting up conferences.

15. Parents who expect too much from their child are sometimes difficult to deal with effectively.

16. Inform the student that you plan to have a conference. At the end of a conference summarize what was agreed to by each party.

17. Remember that it is difficult for parents to be objective about their own children. Criticism will only increase resentment.

Getting Along With Co-Workers

The authors believe that good human relations with co-workers are essential. For example, the basic organization of schools requires teachers to work together, share materials, equipment, and facilities. Failure to establish good working relationship will soon result in problems such as:

1. Lack of cooperation and sharing

2. Petty bickering

3. Poor communication

4. Low morale and a negative climate

Lack of harmony results in duplication of work and an increased burden to the school budget. Inadequate cooperation and sharing requires purchasing additional materials and equipment such as projectors, films and books. This is obviously not a wise use of scarce resources. The most critical aspect of poor human relations among teachers is that it can have a detrimental effect on students. They soon know about the problems listed above and become part of the negative climate. As pointed out in other chapters, good rapport and classroom climate are essential ingredients in the learning process. One of the pitfalls to be avoided is the age old student trap of getting you to listen to their complaints about other teachers. Your answers and actions can do irreparable harm to your rapport with other teachers. It is suggested that you:

1. Listen but do not take sides

2. Tell the student to make an appointment with the other teacher and discuss the matter

3. Be alert for "trap" questions. For example: "Do you think teachers should swear at students?" Obvious answer, "No." Student replies, "Well, Weatherspoon just swore at me." Or, "Do you think it's fair to assign homework tonight when we have homecoming and a dance...?"

4. Report serious complaints to the building administrator who will investigate and keep you uninvolved

Another trap to avoid is blaming administrators or other teachers for your action or inaction. Usually this is the excuse for not allowing students to do something they desire. This problem is even worse when the complaints are aired in public.

Your relationship with other members of your department or grade level are most important. A positive relationship with these individuals can make the difference between liking and disliking teaching.

Many schools use every room every period of the day and this means that during your planning period another teacher must use your room. Problems arise when the regular teacher becomes possessive and will not share with the traveling teacher. Cases have been reported where the regular teacher has even hidden the chalk! When selfishness prevails, students suffer. Don't forget everyone's job is to help educate students - not build empires.

When teachers can't or won't get along, sooner or later the administration will be forced to take action to remedy the situation. All too often this action pleases no one. It is interesting to note that according to U. S. Government statistics, over 80% of employee terminations were caused by poor human relations.

In the final analysis, the best way to get along is to simply follow the Golden Rule. Make an open and honest effort to be cooperative, cordial, and professional at all times. Make a point of always speaking to your colleagues, use good manners, and offer assistance whenever possible.

Remember life is much more pleasant when you enjoy your work and the people with whom you work.

SUMMARY OF SOLUTIONS

1. Make a point of always being friendly, courteous and polite to your co-workers.

2. Never criticize a fellow teacher or administrator in the presence of students or patrons.

3. School facilities, materials, and equipment belong to the general public. Don't make the mistake of becoming possessive.

4. Keep your perspective. Don't become isolated and forget that your classroom and subject is only a part of the total school program.

5. Visit other classes and departments and let others know that you feel their subjects and endeavors are very worthwhile.

6. Happy teachers are generally good teachers. Don't let poor human relations affect your attitude and teaching.

7. Finally -- it is imperative that you get along with others if you wish to be successful in public education.

Orientation of New Students

The mobility of American families has increased dramatically in recent years. This means that large numbers of students are constantly entering and withdrawing during the regular academic year. This phenomena poses may problems for school administrators and classroom teachers. Classroom teachers must familiarize and/or orientate each new student.

Some of the common problems associated with new entries are listed below:

1. Teacher time is required at the expense of the rest of the class.

2. A distraction occurs because the attention of the entire class is focused on the new entry.

3. New students do not arrive at predictable or convenient times. For example, the new entry may arrive after the start of a class period which may also be in the middle of a unit of study or near the end of a grading period.

4. Most new students are completely out of step with the curriculum. They are not familiar with textbooks and other instructional material being used in a particular class.

5. New students are also unfamiliar with classroom procedures and routines.

6. The school building may be a maze or a puzzle for the new student.

7. New students are often misplaced in classes due to insufficient information regarding past achievement and ability.

8. Students are often emotionally upset due to the trauma of leaving their previous school and friends.

In that this problem varies greatly from community to community and even within schools in the same district, teachers must familiarize themselves with the extent of the problem in their school. Assuming this problem exists, you must anticipate and plan so as to minimize the affects of the problems listed above.

So, how are you going to react to the student who just walked into your room with an entry slip? Weatherspoon may respond with "Oh no! Another new student. Stand here, I'll get to you later."

It is hoped that your response will be more humane and that you will consider the student's feelings. Welcome the new student with a smile, explain that you will finish the classroom activities presently underway and then start the orientation procedures.

Hopefully you will have prepared a manual explaining class-room routines, procedures, and policies. Hand this to the new student and request that he read it while waiting. As soon as the lesson permits, quietly explain your orientation procedures to the new entry. Orientation procedures will vary from room to room and also with the particular class or method of instruction. Therefore, consider the following suggestions and choose those that are most appropriate for your particular situation.

1. Autobiographies - many teachers have new students write a short personal history during their first day in class. This enables the teacher to become familiar with the new student's background and the quality of writing will also be an indicator regarding academic achievement and ability.

2. If it is impossible to fit the new student into the present unit of study, you might consider preparing individualized learning activity packages or modules. This will provide a learning experience while waiting for the next unit to begin.

3. Do not record homework or test grades for one or two weeks. This allows time for the student to adjust to the new situation.

4. Find out if one of your students has the same class next period as the new student. Ask this person to show the new student where the room is located.

5. Be careful about introducing the new student to the entire class. Some new students are embarrassed and feel like "a pet on parade".

6. Let the new student know that you are organized. Anticipate new entries by having extra books, book lists, and other instructional materials available.

7. Ensure that you can pronounce the new student's name correctly. Ask what first name or nickname is pre-ferred.

8. Some teachers prefer holding a short after school conference with new students. This is a good time for the teacher to introduce himself and explain his expectations.

9. Place a copy of all handouts, assignments, and other material in a folder. Have new students look through this folder to get a feel for the course.

10. Allow new students to choose where they would like to sit.

11. Keep in mind that new students are new for more than one day. Adjustment may take several weeks.

12. Be aware of the fact that families may not be completely settled in their new homes. Students may not have proper equipment until the family adjustment is completed.

As you can see, there are a variety of ways to orientate a new student. The method you choose must fit your particular subject, your students, and your personality. Develop a procedure which is efficient and the least disruptive to your class. Above all, make sure you anticipate these problems and have an established procedure.

SUMMARY OF SOLUTIONS

1. Please refer to the twelve items listed above.

Traveling Teachers

It is possible that some educators do not know what is meant by the term "traveling teacher". You may have been fortunate enough to have attended a school which could assign each teacher a permanent room. However, many secondary and elementary schools find it necessary to utilize each room every period of the day. Teachers generally have a lunch and planning period every day. There are times that rooms would not be used were it not for traveling teachers. These individuals move from room to room when the regular teacher is not assigned a class in that particular room.

Traveling teachers are confronted with unique problems which are not apparent to a teacher assigned to one room. Consider the average day of one of these unlucky educators:

1. You arrive at school - you may or may not have access to a desk or office.

2. Your materials are either scattered among several rooms or piled on a cart in the faculty lounge.

3. You have not private place to work, meet with students and/or parents.

4. When the school day starts, you find yourself in crowded halls carrying or lugging your materials to your first assigned room.

5. Depending upon the cooperation or attitude of your fellow teacher permanently assigned to a particular room other problems may arise such as: locked desk and supply closet, no chalk and a note complaining about the condition of the room after yesterday's class.

6. Students may have arrived before you and may be out of control due to lack of supervision.

7. At the end of the period, all student contact is severed since you must leave immediately for your next class which may be located at the opposite end of the building.

8. Your day finally ends as it started, in the halls with your hat, coat, and cart and no place to call your own.

These problems vary in their degree of severity depending upon the subject taught, the number of different rooms used, and distance you must travel. The problems cannot be eliminated but can be somewhat alleviated through planning and organization.

You also need the cooperation of the building administrator and your fellow teachers.

It will be very helpful if your rooms are scheduled in one area of the building and not located on different floors. It also helps if you are assigned to rooms that are used for the same subject matter that you teach. For example, it's difficult to teach math in a metal shop.

The building administrator can also help by establishing a positive attitude toward traveling teachers. That is, desks and supplies should be available. The regular teacher should always wait in the room and assist in supervision until the traveling teacher arrives. In fact, permanently assigned teachers must be aware of all problems confronting traveling teachers and be ready and willing to assist whenever possible.

Although planning, organization, and preparation are important for all teachers, it is especially critical for traveling teachers. You must anticipate your needs for the entire day, and if necessary carry everything with you. Request a drawer, shelf, or some space in each room that can be permanently assigned to you. This will help cut down on the amount of material that you need to transport to each class. It may be possible to reserve some wall space or part of a bulletin board in each room. This will help you and your students feel a part of this room and enhance the learning climate.

Students can be helpful by taking your cart or materials to your next class a few minutes before the bell. This will help avoid traveling in crowded halls and also allows time to meet with students after class. Ask your principal to reserve an office or some unassigned area for use before and after school as well as a place for conferences.

You must show a desire to cooperate and work with the permanently assigned teachers. Ask them about materials, supplies, and arrangement of the room. For example, if the chairs are in rows when you arrive, and you move the desks, arrange them back into rows before you leave.

Keep in mind that "traveling" is a necessary evil. A positive attitude on your part will help alleviate many of the above problems. You must make the best of a less than desirable situation.

SUMMARY OF SOLUTIONS

1. Accept the fact that traveling teachers are necessary in schools where sufficient physical space is not available.

2. Teachers should inquire about "traveling" before accepting a new position. You should know all specific policies regarding your assignment.

3. Meet with the regular teachers assigned to your rooms and discuss how you can work harmoniously and cooperate.

4. Regular room teachers should always wait for the traveling teacher to arrive and assist in supervision.

5. Ask your administrator for a desk and filing cabinet. This can be in a classroom, work room, office, or store room.

6. Place all necessary paraphernalia such as grade books, seating charts, and lesson plans in a notebook that goes everywhere with you.

7. Obtain a rolling cart if room assignments are on one floor.

8. Plan your day as if it were a back packing trip.

9. Request that a drawer, a shelf, or some space be permanently assigned to you in each room.

10. Use student aides if a large amount of materials must be transported.

Worry amplfies
a whisper into
a shout
        William Arthur Ward

Chapter VII
ACADEMIC PROBLEMS

Grading Procedures

You may wonder why a discussion of grading procedures is included in a text on classroom management. However, consider the definition of classroom management in the introduction. Classroom management entails anything that is designed to prevent disruption of the educational process.

Grading practices and procedures can and do cause classroom management problems. Please consider the following statements about grades.

1. The process of correcting, recording, making out report cards and progress reports takes a lot of teacher time.

2. Complaints about grades result in more loss of time.
   a) student/teacher conferences
   b) parent conferences
   c) telephone calls to counselors and principals

3. Angry students may become discipline problems.

4. Students categorize teachers as being unfair, too hard or too easy.

5. Parents and students may request schedule changes.

6. Students may choose to drop classes and lose credit.

7. Grades determine scholarships and entrance to some colleges.

8. Grades cause turmoil in homes between parents and children.

9. Grades are often interpreted as "like" or "dislike" by students.

10. Poor grades may destroy the self-esteem of students.

11. Students may learn to dislike certain subjects due to poor grades.

The above incidents all take time and effort to resolve. Therefore, you have less time for productive planning and organization of lessons. These problems also result in some alienation among teachers, parents and students. This negative behavior may lead to additional management problems.

All too often students and parents don't understand grading procedures. Some students still feel that teachers "give" them a grade - that is, it is not earned. Some students and parents believe grades are based upon some mysterious or personal whim of teachers. When students and parents don't understand your grading system you are open to many accusations.

Like many of us, when students don't understand the system they feel it is unfair. Students must understand the reward system (grades) if you expect them to be motivated and work hard. A secretive or highly complex grading system may also result in a loss of student teacher rapport and trust. Again, this may increase your classroom discipline problems.

Most of these problems occur because of the extreme variance and inconsistency in grading procedures. Not only do grading systems vary from district to district but even within the same building you will find very different methods of computing grades. The problem is further compounded when teachers at the same grade level and/or subject use totally different methods to arrive at a grade. This, in effect, can create two different classes out of what is the same class. The only variable becomes the teacher.

Other problems created by inconsistency are as follows:

1. Some teachers grade in relation to student ability while others grade on absolute achievement.

2. Some teachers grade on a curve or in relationship to the rest of the class while some do not.

3. Methods of weighing test scores, homework, classwork, and special projects varies among teachers.

4. Some teachers decide in advance as to how grades will be distributed while others do not.

5. Some teachers consider classroom behavior while others do not.

6. Some teachers' grade books are secretive while others are not.

7. Some teachers allow extra credit while others do not.

8. Some schools use weighted grades with variable grade points based on the difficulty of the class while most do not.

9. A student with five or six different teachers may have to learn five of six different grading procedures.

10. Academic requirements may vary among the same classes with different teachers.

It is unfortunate, but factual, that a student's grade often is determined by "who" teaches the class as much as by the quality and quantity of his work. To prove this point, the authors have devised an exercise in grading. This exercise has been used with over 200 teachers. Teachers representing several grade levels and subjects were given four identical examples of student work. The student work consisted of two quizzes, one term paper, and a final test. Correct answers were supplied. Teachers were asked to assign a letter grade to each paper and then compute a term grade based upon the four papers. Results on individual papers varied from "F" to "A" and the term grade from "D" to "A". As you can see, the only variable was the teacher. Obviously, different methods and standards were used to compute the grades.

The authors feel that an effective grading system should include the following characteristics:

1. Easily understood by parents, students and other educators

2. Simple to compute

3. Open and non-secretive

4. Objective rather than subjective

5. Consistent

6. Based on numerous assignments, quizzes or tests

A highly successful method of grading is the "point system". This method allows teachers to assign a variable number of points to different items such as homework, quizzes, major tests and projects.

A percentage can easily be obtained by comparing the total possible points to the pupil's earned points. This type of grading system is much like computing a "batting average" and is relatively easy for students to understand. Teachers can go one step further and encourage or require students to keep a record of their grades and progressive averages.

This method also allows teachers to easily communicate with parents when explaining grades. It is further suggested that you

85

require students to keep a record of their grades. A simple chart can suffice, such as the one below:

Nature of Work	Date	Possible Points	My Points	% on This Assignment	Cumulative Average
Home-work	3/10	5	4	80%	80%
Quiz	3/15	10	8	80%	80%
Unit Test	3/20	50	45	90%	88%

You may also enhance communications with parents by going beyond the traditional report card which usually only lists a letter grade. You might consider compiling an additional or supplementary report which shows a student's total points, percent, and rank in class. A sample chart is provided below.

Total possible points - 1000

POINTS	PERCENTAGE	NUMBER OF STUDENTS
990	99%	1
960	96%	4
950	95%	2
.	.	.
.	.	.
.	.	.
840	84%	5 John Doe

Letter Grade_____B_____
Class Rank_____12_____

Parental Signature

_____

As you can see, this supplementary sheet provides parents with much additional information. Encourage students to take the report home and discuss it with their parents. An incentive of a few extra credit points may help achieve this goal.

Your grading procedure should also include methods of keeping parents informed between reporting periods. Do not hesitate to call parents, have conferences, send home progress reports, or "happy grams". Parents do not like to be surprised when report cards are issued.

The above procedures will insure that parents are kept informed at all times and students always know where they stand.

SUMMARY OF SOLUTIONS

1. Make sure students thoroughly understand your grading system.

2. Ensure that you feel comfortable with your grading system.

3. Do not be secretive or mysterious.

4. Allow students to come in after school and see and discuss their grades.

5. Go over grades with students before report cards are issued.

6. Use objective criteria whenever possible.

7. Use as simple a grading system as possible.

8. Do not allow discipline to affect academic grades.

9. Require students to keep a record of their own grades.

10. Be open minded enough to "curve grades" when your teaching or tests may have been the cause of low grades. Ask yourself the following questions:

    a) Did you adequately cover all material?
    b) Did you clearly tell the students what they were responsible for knowing?
    c) Did you review?
    d) Were the test questions clear?
    e) Were the directions clear?
    f) Was the test legible and readable?
    g) Did students have enough time?
    h) Did your best students earn an "A"?

11. Prepare frequency distribution curves of your grades. Try to ascertain if your grades are consistent with standardized student test scores.

12. Compare your grades with teachers teaching the same subject and grade level.

13. Try to avoid testing on Fridays. Students often have to cope with several tests on the same day.

Individualization

Many secondary school teachers have upwards of 150 to 200 different students in their classes every day. Suggestions to individualize are usually met with a response such as: "Why – kids are kids"; "How"; "I have too many students"; or "I don't have the time". There is no question that large numbers of students and the time schedule of secondary schools may make individualizing difficult. Another part of the problem is the traditional overemphasis of the lecture in secondary classrooms. Apparently, many secondary teachers believe that lectures and discussions are the only methods of teaching.

The fact is, students differ. The average heterogenious class will have tremendous differences in achievement and ability levels. Subject matter oriented teachers tend to teach to the middle or high ability level students. Where does this leave the young person who is a poor reader, one who is very bright, or has some type of educational handicap? Remember, a discipline problem is usually a student who is not having his needs met.

Most states encourage educators to develop each student to his/her highest potential. Teachers have an ethical and moral responsibility to do the best they can for each and every student. In consideration of the problems already cited, how can this be done? There are many simple and painless techniques that any classroom teacher can put into effect which will result in individualization.

Prior to implementing any particular teaching technique, it is imperative to know the strengths and weaknesses of your students. To obtain this information you may wish to investigate the following sources:

1. Cumulative folders.

2. Permanent record cards

3. Diagnostic tests

4. Other teachers

5. Special services, i.e., counselor, nurse, etc.

6. Questioning techniques

7. Autobiographies

8. Pre and post tests

With this information in hand, you will be aware of the individual differences present within your classroom. Awareness is the first step toward meeting the individual needs of your students.

Other techniques which you may wish to consider are:

1. Ask questions which are directly related to student abilities

2. Develop projects and assignments around student interests

3. Always read tests and worksheets orally

4. Differentiate tests to include recognition and recall as well as mastery questions (thought questions or essay). Slower students will have success with matching questions while thought questions will challenge bright students.

5. Student contracts

6. Individual assignments (independent study)

7. Learning centers

This is, of course, only a partial list of the techniques which may be used. A truly professional teacher will constantly search for successful methods of individualization.

It should also be pointed out that many behavior problems can be avoided through individualization. This is why this section is included in a book on classroom management.

SUMMARY OF SOLUTIONS

1. Know strengths and weaknesses of your students.

2. Consult records, guidance personnel, and other teachers.

3. Use "learning style" questionnaires to identify the learning styles of your students. Adapt your instructional techniques to each student's peculiar learning style.

4. Make sure poor students experience success.

5. Use student aides to assist poorer students during work periods.

6. Examine the rate at which you cover material. Use questions to determine if students are keeping pace.

7. Face the fact that all students can't do the same amount of work in terms of quality and quantity. Vary your expectations and requirements in terms of student abilities.

8. Use as many different teaching methods as you can think of in order to reach all students.

Homework and Assignments

There are generally two ways homework can cause problems for classroom teachers. The least obvious problem is when all students do their homework on a regular basis and you become inundated with papers to correct. Teachers need to be careful not to assign too much homework and create situations where they simply don't have time to adequately correct assignments. Often this time could be better spent preparing lessons or working individually with students. A wise teacher can easily overcome this problem.

However, the other major problem is not as easily controlled. Sometimes students simply do not complete assignments. This can be a form of defiance and lead to more serious classroom discipline problems. You obviously want to avoid this type of situation. Let's examine some reasons students fail to do homework.

In many cases the reason is similar to the teacher's problem described above, that is, students simply do not have time to do the assignments for all teachers. Remember, your students may have several other classes, all of which may assign homework.

Another reason students fail to do homework is that they are bored with the assignment. Homework assignments need to be meaningful, have a purpose, and somehow relate to the student's life.

To maintain student interest you might ask yourself some questions concerning your homework assignments. Do your assignments consider differing abilities and interests of students, and are they geared to their interests and abilities? If not, why not? It is also important for students to understand the reason for doing assignments. Are you excited and enthused about your class and the homework? Or like Weatherspoon, will you blame the students - stating that they get lazier every year?

All too often homework is what is commonly called "busy work". Assignments should always be a learning experience and reinforce your classroom lessons. Don't let your assignments become repetitious "busy work" for students who have already mastered the skill or concept being taught.

Do you always correct and return assignments within a reasonable length of time? Or do you dispose of student work in the trash can? The quality and quantity of student work in your class will be directly related to your method of reward and reinforcement. Students will soon develop the same attitude toward homework that you display.

How do you go about giving a homework assignment? Do you have an established procedure or do you shout out tomorrow's assignment as the bell is ringing and students are dashing out the door. You should establish a procedure for assigning homework. Always ensure that the assignment is thoroughly understood by all students. This necessitates both oral and written directions with adequate time for questions and working examples.

Let's examine a couple of methods for handling homework which will not take up most of your evening to correct. First, remember "Ebbinghouses' Curve for Learning" which states that most people learn a little at a time. Therefore, teach a little at a time.

Why collect homework at all? Why not give an assignment such as learn the information on pages 26-27? Next day give a quiz. You may increase student attentiveness by giving a quiz at the end of the period. This, by the way, cuts down discipline problems, motivates students to pay attention and makes life more pleasant.

When you find that some students aren't doing what you expect, after you've tried every method you know, don't blame them or yourself. Remember, students are people. Some teachers are satisfied with being poor or mediocre teachers and some students are satisfied with a "C", while others want only to be the best.

SUMMARY OF SOLUTIONS

1. Make relevant assignments which are meaningful to students.

2. Give students sufficient time to properly complete assignments.

3. Be cognizant of the fact that your students have other classes.

4. Explain why certain assignments are necessary.

5. Correct and return homework promptly.

6. The teacher's attitude toward homework will directly affect student motivation.

7. Your procedure for giving assignments should include oral and written directions with sufficient time for questions. Allow classtime to start homework assignments. This will take care of any misunderstandings.

8. Be aware that homework often reflects the work of others, i.e., friends and parents. Grades should be weighed with this in mind.

9. Ensure that adequate resources are available for students to complete assignments.

10. Require all students to complete and turn in all assignments. Students should report to your room after school and complete unfinished assignments.

11. Notify parents by letter or phone if students do not do required work.

12. Test students over homework assignments rather than grading the actual assignment. This will require learning and decrease cheating.

13. Homework assignments don't have to be written work. Assignments can be to learn certain information.

14. Don't assign homework as "punishment".

15. Examine the amount of time you and your students spend on homework or seat work. Are there better ways of learning the same material? For example, drill and review may result in more learning than seat work.

16. It is not necessary to correct and grade all homework. Give a small number of points for simply completing and handing in the assignment. Tests will indicate learning or lack of learning.

17. Don't flounder over late assignments. Establish a rule that assignments are worth so many points when on time and so many points when late.

Class Size

There is a direct relationship between the frequency and severity of discipline problems and the number of students in a classroom. McPortland concluded when over thirty students are in a class the teacher spends in inordinate amount of time maintaining control and correspondingly less time on instruction. 1/ The February, 1979 issue of the Kappan reported ... "As class size decreases, student achievement climbs, particularly when size goes below twenty students ..." 2/ In a similar study for American Educational Research Association, Cahen and Filby found that classroom management and discipline were better when teachers had fewer students. 3/

It is also interesting to note that various psychological studies on "crowding" indicate increased stress and anxiety often lead to misbehavior. A NIE-NSOE study concluded that large classes experience more violence and vandalism. 4/

The obvious answer is to have larger classrooms with fewer students per class. However, the physical plant and personnel available is controlled by a school district's budget. Most school districts throughout the country simply do not have the funds to reduce class size. Therefore, you will probably face larger classes than research indicates is desirable.

You must be much better prepared and probably more structured when you face a large class. Instructions must be concise and easily understood. Insure that students understand why you're less permissive than you may wish to be. These actions will help students recognize the problem. Even normal student movement in a large class may cause a high noise level.

Change the searing arrangement of your room. Some arrangements give the appearance of being less crowded while still allowing freedom of movement. You also need to adapt your teaching style to class size. For example, large classes and small rooms do not lend themselves to group activities or laboratory experiments.

Maintain a positive attitude when faced with the problems of large classes. A negative attitude almost ensures difficulties. You may not be able to control class size but you must be able to control what happens in your class.

SUMMARY OF SOLUTIONS

1. Large classes mandate structure and organization.

2. Minimize student movement.

3. Store equipment and supplies in other areas when not in use to best utilize available space.

4. Use a seating arrangement that take up the least amount of space.

5. Maintain a positive attitude and explain to your students why your classroom management procedures differ from those used in smaller classes.

6. Research indicates that students will not benefit from reduced class size if teachers continue to use the same instructional techniques in smaller classes that they use in larger classes. 5/

1/ James McPortland and McDill, Ed., "High School Rules and Decision Making." Baltimore: John Hopkins Press, Feb., 1974.

2/ "Newsfront," Kappan, February, 1979.

3/ Ibid.

4/ NIE-NSOE Monogram, February, 1978.

5/ Summary and Conclusions - Class Size, a Summary of Research, Educational Research Service, Inc., Arlington, Virginia, 1978.

Today's

decisions

are

tommorow's

realities

Dr. Robert H. Schuller

Chapter VIII
SUPERVISORY RESPONSIBILITIES

Leaving Your Classroom unsupervised

Vandalism, injuries, theft, and other destructive acts take place in unsupervised instructional settings. In other words, a group of students are present in a classroom without a teacher.

These unsupervised situations come about for a variety of reasons. Some examples of why teachers are not in the classroom are listed below:

1. A trip to the restroom

2. An emergency phone call

3. Need for instructional materials

4. Cigarette and/or coffee break

5. Socialization with other staff members

6. Being late to class

As you can see, some reasons are more valid than others.

Regardless of the reason, problems often occur when the teacher is out of the room. Students often become noisy and begin moving around the room. Depending upon the students and the teacher, this may evolve into a very disruptive situation. Irresponsible students will begin talking loudly and shouting. Shoving and fighting may result in student injury or damage to the classroom. This is especially critical in classes where potentially dangerous equipment is present. However, injuries may occur in any room.

The problems associated with unsupervised classes may be further complicated by legal action. Courts have ruled that teachers are negligent and therefore liable for damages when students under their supervision are left alone. This is especially true when teachers are out of the classroom for reasons such as a cigarette or coffee break.

Teachers must anticipate and plan so as to reduce or eliminate the reasons for leaving a class unsupervised. Make sure that you have all necessary equipment and instructional materials in your room before class begins. However, if you err, send a student aide to obtain needed items rather than leaving the classroom. In most schools, office secretaries will reproduce materials for you as long as it does not become habitual.

If a situation arises which requires you to leave the room, ask the teacher next door to help supervise your class. You can also stop by the lounge, workroom, or office and ask a fellow teacher who is unassigned at that time to cover your class.

If you are fortunate enough to have a public address call back system in your room, notify the office that you are leaving so they can monitor your room. The office can also initiate this procedure if they are calling you out of the room.

A prudent teacher will also establish classroom procedures that students will follow when the teacher is out of the room. For example, absolutely no talking or leaving your seat.

As with nearly all classroom management problems, prior anticipation and planning will reduce your absences from the classroom. This will also diminish the possibility of accidents or incidents occurring when you must be out of the room.

SUMMARY OF SOLUTIONS

1. Proper planning and anticipation of needs will reduce or eliminate the necessity of leaving a room unsupervised.

2. Ask fellow teachers to supervise your room if it is necessary to leave.

3. Notify the office of your situation.

4. Prepare your students for unsupervised situations with specific procedures to be followed.

5. Never forget your legal responsibilities regarding supervision.

6. Always lock your classroom door during recess, planning period, or lunch. This prevents unsupervised students from entering your room.

7. Many problems occur during passing periods when teachers are down the hall or in the restroom. Stand by your door in a position to observe both the hall and your classroom.

Hall Supervision

Have you ever visited a school during a change of classes when teachers did not help with hall supervision? If so, you probably observed one or more of the following: running, pushing, fighting, shouting, vandalism, or in short general mayhem.

You may be asking yourself why this topic is included in this book since coverage has been limited to classroom problems. When students are allowed to become unruly in the halls, it will carry over into your classroom. Then you must spend valuable classroom time restoring order. Not only do you expend time but it also takes energy which could be better spent with classroom instruction.

You may have heard that teachers are employed to teach - not supervise the halls. However, administrators cannot be everywhere at once. If supervision breaks down the school will soon be controlled by the unruly. Halls will not be a safe place for the majority of students. It is literally impossible to have chaos in the halls and order in the classroom. A cooperative program of control by all school employees is advocated.

Teachers should stand by their classroom door so they can observe the hall and the classroom. Your presence alone will eliminate most serious hall problems. Furthermore, you should dismiss your class from the door and greet the next class from the same position. Remember, bells only remind you that the period is over - teachers dismiss classes.

There are many reasons for standing by the door and a couple of the most obvious are:

1. When a class is dismissed properly, students leave in an orderly manner.

2. It gives you the opportunity to talk to students as they leave and enter.

A legitimate question might be, "What do I do when I observe unruly behavior in the halls?" All too often students are immediately sent to the principal. Why not stop the student and in a friendly manner state that he seems tired from rushing and needs a rest. Talk to him a minute and let him go. The student knows he was wrong and will respect you for not sending him to the principal.

Some administrators are insuring that teachers fully understand school rules and policies prior to signing the initial contract. Many administrators ask how you feel about supervising halls and taking part in school activities. Administrators recognize there are many reasons which may prevent a teacher from being in the hall between every class. It is suggested that you keep these absences to an absolute minimum to ensure adequate hall supervision.

Remember, it is much easier to prevent problems than it is to cure them.

SUMMARY OF SOLUTIONS

1. Recognize the fact that teaching responsibilities do not begin and end at the classroom door.

2. Dismiss classes from the door and remain in that position between classes.

3. Remind students in the halls to move along and not run and push.

4. Refer chronic offenders to the principal.

5. The presence of a teacher prevents problems.

Checking the Bathroom

School restrooms are used for many reasons other than the obviously designated purpose. For example, restrooms are often the gathering place for groups of students. These students choose to meet in restrooms because of the privacy afforded. These meetings require privacy because violations of school regulations often are involved.

For example, restrooms are the most commonly used places for smoking. Restrooms are also an excellent place for the use or distribution of controlled substances.

Smoking and the use of drugs often lead to other problems. Wastebaskets often catch on fire. Vandalism results as sinks are torn from the wall, mirrors broken, and paper dispensers destroyed. As you can see, incidents of this type also set the stage for fights, assaults, and extortion.

The previously described incidents affect the total school climate and more specifically, the learning environment in your classroom. Tardiness increases because these students often need more time than allowed during a passing period. Some students may arrive in class under the influence.

Students who do not take part in these activities also suffer. They become afraid to enter restrooms as they fear for their personal safety or do not wish to be associated with illegal acts. If these students cannot use restrooms during the passing periods, they will probably request a restroom pass during class. This further disrupts your class activities.

All of these problems occur due to insufficient supervision of restrooms. Most schools have more restrooms than administrators. Therefore, it is obvious that the building principals cannot do the job by themselves. Administrators need the assistance of the teaching staff. The problem is further compounded if administrators are all of the same sex and therefore are prevented from checking restrooms of the other sex.

Students soon identify which restrooms are unsupervised, and will congregate in these areas. Teachers can alleviate these problems by actually walking in and out of restrooms on a regular basis. It also helps if teachers are in the halls near restrooms during passing periods. Students will be less destructive knowing that a teacher is outside the door.

The problems associated with the use of restroom passes during class periods is discussed in another section of this book. (See Bathroom Charlie) It is obvious that teachers must develop procedures which restrict and prevent the abuse of the restroom privilege.

The safety and well being of students must be the concern of all school employees. Inasmuch as some school restrooms have become dangerous areas, it follows that everyone must assist to alleviate this problem.

SUMMARY OF SOLUTIONS

1. Walk in and out of restrooms whenever possible.

2. Position yourself near restrooms when supervising halls.

3. If a student is observed violating school rules, personally escort the student to the building principal.

Non-Classroom Assignments

Most teachers have assigned duties other than classroom instruction. Examples of these supervisory duties are:

1. Lunchroom

2. Playground

3. Hall

4. Study Hall

5. Loading and unloading busses

6. Crowd control for activities

The number and types of non-classroom duties varies among regions of the country and schools. In all cases, teachers are assigned a minimum amount of time in which they must be engaged in the supervision of students - either in or out of a classroom.

Problems encountered in non-classroom assignments generally are quite different than those experienced in a classroom. You are often dealing with large groups in a relatively unstructured setting with students whom you are not familiar. Picture a lunchroom or playground teeming with active and noisy adolescents. It should be obvious that you cannot supervise these situations in the same manner you would a classroom of thirty students.

Keep the rules and procedures as simple as possible. Excessively complex regulations often result in unnecessary harassment and alienation of students. Remember, for many students, these are periods of relaxation, social interaction, and a time to unwind or let off steam. Students expect, demand, and deserve more freedom while in the halls, at lunch, or on the playground. After all, as a teacher, you want students to arrive in your classroom in a receptive and positive frame of mind.

The basic rules should center around student safety, physical damage of facilities, and to prevent disruption of other classes. The most important aspect of this type of supervision is being visible. Your physical presence will deter most undesirable acts. Be patient, wait and observe actual violations of rules before taking any action. Impulsive reactions will often place teachers in "no-win" situations.

The way in which you conduct yourself while engaged in non-classroom duties may adversely or positively affect your relationship with students in your classroom. Wandering around

103

halls, lunchrooms, or playgrounds can be an excellent opportunity to establish rapport with students. Use these times for friendly chatter and interactions.

SUMMARY OF SOLUTIONS

1. Being visible to students prevents problems.

2. Discipline students only when the incident involves safety, harassment of others, or damage to facilities.

3. Avoid open confrontations with students and handle the problems in private.

4. Use supervision periods to establish rapport with students. This will help when problems arise.

5. Don't harass students, but do observe quietly and openly.

6. Move around the entire area under your supervision. Don't stay in one place.

Chapter IX
CONFRONTATIONS WITH STUDENTS

Defiance

Most beginning and many veteran teachers worry or at least wonder what they will do if a student defies them. What will you do if you ask a student to pick up a piece of papers which was dropped on the floor and he responds with "Stick it in your ear!", or worse? You had better have some plan of action, because when these things happen the adrenaline starts pumping, and your ability to think clearly is greatly diminished. Let's examine two types of defiance most often encountered in classrooms.

OVERT DEFIANCE

Overt defiance is open or active disobedience which is a direct challenge to you. It may take any number of forms including swearing or physical attack upon your person.

Many, if not all open acts of defiance can be prevented. Teachers don't knowingly back themselves into corners but may not be aware of the outcomes of their acts. Some teachers cause problems by unwittingly making unwise decisions or using poor judgment. For example, statements made in anger, such as, "You'll have to stay in all week," or "Sit on the floor," may provoke a student to overt defiant action. Threatening statements made in front of peers is considered a "put-down" and usually results in some form of immediate response.

You probably will not have this problem if you make reasonable requests. All teachers know they should not punish the entire class for the actions of a few, but in times of stress it is very easy to act unwisely.

When an incident occurs in the classroom and the offender is unknown, all too often the following happens. Teacher, "Who did that?" The response is silence. Teacher, "All right, who did that?" More silence. Teacher, "Until the scoundrel who did that admits it or someone tells me who did it, everyone will remain after class."

You have now put yourself in a "no-win" situation. You're asking for someone to admit guilt or inform on someone else in front of his peers and you're going to punish the entire class for the actions of one person. Then your best student says, "I didn't do it, and I have a dental appointment." She gets up and walks out. Do you see the position you have placed yourself into? What if everyone walks out except the student who committed the act? The student says, "I did it, and I'm sorry." You now know who committed the act but have lost your authority and the respect of the entire class.

You do not wish to make the preceding mistakes. A more reasonable approach to this problem may be to avoid a scene if at all possible. Take whatever action is necessary to immediately handle the problem. That is, tone it down or buy time so you can deal with the situation in a private and calm manner.

Defiance should never be tolerated by any teacher. Assuming you have made a reasonable request, what then do you do with a defiant student?

The severity of the defiant act should dictate your immediate action. For example, a minor act may be ignored for the moment and handled later. A slightly more serious offense can be handled by saying, "See me after class" and immediately go on with the lesson.

Defiant acts are disruptive to the learning process and embarrassing to teachers and other members of the class. These acts may call for immediate removal of that individual from the classroom. This removal may take the form of sending the student into the hallway, to the office, or calling a building adminis-trator. If you have an intercom, use it. Firmly state that an administrator is needed in room 117 immediately. If an intercom is not available, send a note with your most trustworthy student.

Never lay a hand on a student under these conditions. It is too easy to strike a student. By not losing your temper and acting as an adult, the students will respect you. Remember it is just too easy to lose your temper under this type of stress. Also, courts are reluctant to uphold educators when corporal punishment is administered in the heat of anger.

COVERT DEFIANCE

Covert defiance is usually very subtle and often can be more difficult to deal with than overt defiance. The following subtle acts are examples of covert behavior:

1. Asking irrelevant questions

2. Glaring at the teacher

3. Unresponsiveness or "I don't know"

4. Sly sneers

5. Intentionally responding very slowly to reasonable requests

106

6. Coughing or laughing

7. Exaggerated response to teacher requests

8. Wearing inappropriate attire

9. Asking questions to which the teacher may not know the answer

As you can see, the preceding acts themselves would require no discipline. Yet, they are of the nature to cause teachers many sleepless nights trying to think of a way to overcome the problem.

These acts may really "get under your skin". Unless they are disrupting the learning process, it may be better to ignore them.

When action is necessary, your choice will be determined by your personality, school rules, and the severity of the problem.

1. Have a private conference with the student and attempt to find out why he acts as he does

2. Call home. (Refer to section on calling parents)

3. Consult with and/or refer student to the counselor

4. Completely ignore the student

5. Compliment his positive actions

6. Try joking with students to get compliance

Keep in mind that occasionally a severe personality conflict between student and teacher does occur. Most administrators do not expect teachers to have perfect rapport with all students. Therefore, do not hesitate to refer the student to a counselor or administrator for possible transfer to another class. When this occurs only occasionally, it does not diminish your stature as a professional educator.

When dealing with this most stressing problem, remember that some people have an "authority phobia". That is, they resent anyone in authority. Recognize that challenge is a natural part of maturation but do encourage students to challenge in a positive manner. Some students may need special counseling. All students need to be made aware of your expectations. Remember a polite and courteous request usually results in a positive response.

107

SUMMARY OF SOLUTIONS

1. Do not make unreasonable requests which you cannot enforce.

2. Deal with problems privately.

3. The severity of defiant acts should dictate your actions.

4. Never strike a student.

5. Refer possible personality conflicts to a counselor or the building administrator.

6. Don't challenge students in front of their peers.

7. Never ignore acts of defiance but carefully choose your battle ground.

8. In open confrontations, allow students to "save face", yet obey.

9. Polite and courteous requests will help avoid defiant acts.

10. Don't give final ultimatums which lead to open confrontations.

11. Don't surprise students with new rules.

12. Allow students adequate time to obey a teacher request.

13. Use a calm tone of voice when asking a student to comply with a request.

14. Avoid direct orders whenever possible. Use words like "would you mind" or "I'd appreciate it if you would" when speaking to a student. This prevents you from being placed in a "no-win" situation.

Fights and Altercations

Any experienced classroom teacher will agree that most students have social problems. Unfortunately, adolescents do not have the maturity level or social skills necessary to handle these problems as well as most adults. When disagreements occur among young people, they all too often lead to noisy bickering, wrangling, and frequently physical altercation. These types of conflicts are obviously disruptive forces with which educators must deal.

You must anticipate the possibility of student conflict and plan procedures and strategies to deal with the problem. When a fight breaks out in your class, it is too late to begin planning a course of action.

As stated in other sections, during the first few days of school ensure that your students understand your expectations. In this case, let students know that they are to leave problems such as the ones described above outside the classroom. Explain that you will not tolerate wasting class time listening to personal arguments or bickering.

If verbal conflicts do occur, stop them immediately. If this cannot be accomplished by simply telling them to stop, then separate the antagonists. This can be done by changing seats, moving to the hall, or sending to the office. You simply cannot afford to waste the time of the entire class due to an argument involving a few students.

Encourage students who are having conflicts to visit with you after school. If this doesn't help, refer them to the guidance office. Students need to learn the necessary social skills which will enable them to solve personal conflicts without resorting to bitter arguments or actual physical fights.

What if a physical fight does occur in your classroom? What would you do? All too often teachers get in the middle to break up the fight. You can get injured! What if someone hits you and you retaliate? You're then in trouble besides being injured.

You can try yelling at them to stop. At the same time send a trusted student to the office to get help from school administrators. If you have a P. A. system with a call back device, by all means use it.

You may be able to call upon the teacher next door for assistance. Often if two teachers grab each combatant from behind they will stop.

You must consider all the possible ramifications of your action or inaction including the following:

1. Your own size and strength

2. Age and size of the students

3. Are they using fists or weapons

Hopefully you will never have to confront a problem like this but you should be ready with a plan of action.

SUMMARY OF SOLUTIONS

1. At the beginning of the school year explain to your students the difference between petty and serious problems.

2. Petty problems will not be allowed in the classroom.

3. Serious problems should be reported to a teachers, counselor, or administrator in private.

4. Students who do not get along should be separated.

5. When fights do occur, refer to the last paragraph in this section.

6. Conduct a private conference with students who are not getting along.

7. Insist that students keep their hands to themselves. Many fights are the direct result of immature actions such as grabbing, poking, tripping, etc. Sooner or later someone gets mad and a physical altercation results.

8. Tell students not to believe second hand information from friends regarding possible altercations. Many fights are literally started by "promoters" who serve as friends to both antagonists.

9. Identify your classroom or school "bully" early in the year. Refer such students to the principal.

10. Be alert for intimidated students. Fear and anxiety will reflect in their school work and possibly in their attendance. Such students should be referred to counselors or principals.

11. Report all rumors of possible after school fights to an administrator immediately. In many cases, action can be taken to prevent a possibly serious fight.

12. Teachers should expect a certain amount of "wrangling" among students as students do not possess the social skills and maturity to handle problems in an adult manner. However, do not waste valuable class time on such problems. Refer to the proper school personnel.

Verbal and Physical Abuse of Teachers

The type, amount, and severity of verbal abuse varies depending upon geographic location, such as, metropolitan or rural; or from one school to another within the same district; or for that matter, among different teachers in the same school.

What is meant by verbal abuse? Some examples are:

1. Students cursing or swearing at teachers

2. Disrespectful gestures or facial expressions

3. Open threats or other forms of intimidation

4. Disrespectful or obscene nicknames or words with double meanings

5. Sexual overtones

6. Phone calls late at night or on weekends

7. Irate comments from parents or patrons during phone calls or conferences

Regardless of the type or source of abuse, it usually follows some type of teacher/student/parent confrontation. Typically, some disciplinary action has been administered by the teacher and the verbal abuse is an attempt at retaliation. Fortunately, this type of problem occurs infrequently, at least in the author's experience.

In an attempt to avoid the unpleasantness inherent in the above situations, some teachers overlook violations of verbal abuse. Some students are quick to identify teachers of this type and prey upon this weak trait. Unfortunately, the problems get worse rather than better.

Teachers also are confronted with verbal abuse outside of the regular classroom. For example, it is not uncommon to hear snide or obscene remarks while walking down a crowded hallway. It is very difficult to identify the source of such remarks. Overreaction without proof can further compound the problem. The same problems also occur in places like school cafeterias or while attending school activities. Unfortunately, teachers sometimes suffer verbal abuse in non-school settings such as shopping centers or recreational areas.

Regardless of the type of verbal abuse or where it occurs it is extremely disconcerting. The recipient of the abuse usually becomes very upset or angry, attempts to identify the source of

112

the abusive language, and then takes punitive action. The authors advise caution. Over reaction may compound the problem. Above all, do not retaliate with physical force, more abusive language, or lose your temper. Your reaction may determine the frequency of these incidents. People generally cease name-calling if the desired response is not obtained. In all cases, remain calm, identify the source if possible, and report the incident to the proper authority. In short, act as if the incident does not bother you, but take decisive action whenever possible.

Be especially careful when dealing with incidents involving students who seem to be irrational or "out-of-control". These cases could involve the use of drugs, alcohol, or an emotionally disturbed student. (See section on drugs and mental illness.) Verbal abuse can easily evolve into physical abuse. Don't take any action which will tend to increase the level of violence.

Like verbal abuse, physical abuse of teachers varies considerably in its degree of severity. It may be just a bump in the hall, a student jerking, pushing, hitting, or in extreme cases can involve the use of a weapon. Thankfully, the latter rarely occurs.

Similar courses of action are advised for physical and verbal abuse. Ignore unintentional acts or those which cannot be proven. Never ignore an intentional act and always report the incident to the building administrator. If you feel your personal well being is in imminent danger, defend yourself in an appropriate manner.

As with all classroom management problems, the frequency of verbal and physical abuse varies considerably among teachers. Some teachers have a great deal of trouble with verbal and/or physical abuse while others rarely experience this problem. The authors suggest that there may be a high correlation between the use of positive classroom management techniques and the way you are treated by students.

SUMMARY OF SOLUTIONS

1. Do not overlook abusive acts.

2. Do not overreact and compound the problem. Do not lose your temper.

3. Identify the source of verbal abuse and conduct a private conference or make a referral to an administrator.

4. Refer all cases of physical abuse to an administrator.

5. Avoid derogatory comments to students since such acts often result in similar responses from students.

6. The use of physical force should be avoided when disciplining students.

7. Verbal abuse from students often follows a loud verbal admonition of a student in a public setting. Avoid verbal admonitions in the presence of other students and you will decrease the likelihood of retaliation from students.

Chapter X
KNOWING SCHOOL POLICIES

Board Policy and Faculty Guides

The majority of school districts have developed and make available some or all of the following items:

1. Board Policy Manual
2. Faculty Handbook
3. Student Handbook
4. Curriculum Guides
5. Negotiation Agreement

6. Administrative Procedures
7. Weekly Bulletins
8. Faculty Meetings
9. P. A. Announcements
10. Bulletin Boards

These guides and manuals are a school district's policies and procedures. Every employee is expected to understand and abide by these policies. This may seem an overwhelming task for a new teachers in a strange community. However, you may find yourself facing a multitude of problems if you do not become familiar with these policies. Let's examine some of these problems.

One of the most obvious problems may be ignorance of emergency procedures such as fire drills and accidents. The ramifications of not knowing policies in these types of cases may involve student injury and possible legal action.

Another problem of not knowing policies involves your relationship with students, other educators, and parents. These groups are very sensitive to inconsistent enforcement of policies. Some groups may even come to resent you. For example students may ask, "Why can't we do it in here, Mrs. B. lets us do it in her classroom?' Students may not be the only group to become confused and resentful. Other faculty members may confront you for not enforcing policy.

Adolescents have a difficult enough time adjusting to life. They do not need great variance from room to room. In many cases, students know procedures better than teachers, especially new teachers. This may stem from the fact that a student may have been in the system much longer than a new teacher. New teachers have not had the experience of being involved in the development of existing policies. Regardless, students do not respect a teacher's ignorance of procedures.

An old saying is "Ignorance of the law is no excuse". This may also apply to school district policies. If you consistently ignore district policies, your action may be construed as insubordination. You should know that insubordination is cause for dismissal in most states.

You may not agree with some district policies. However, the fact that you accepted employment means you have agreed to abide by district policies. If you feel changes should be made, check your district's procedures for changing policies.

The answer to these potential problems is obvious - read and understand all policy manuals. Do not accept or rely on word of mouth interpretations of policies. If you have questions consult with your building administrator.

SUMMARY OF SOLUTIONS

1. Read and understand all policy manuals.

2. Review and refer to policies prior to making major decisions.

3. Consult with administrators to clarify questions.

4. A large number of classroom and school management problems would be avoided through compliance with the three suggestions listed above.

5. Many poor teacher evaluations and/or dismissals are the direct result of teachers not following established policies. Follow policies regardless of your personal opinions and work through proper channels to instigate desired changes.

Student Appearance

Student fads such as dress, hairstyles, and other customs are in a constant state of flux. These changes in appearance sometimes affect the way students behave and may be perceived as immoral or indecent. Teachers must be alert for new modes of dress whenever they affect the classroom learning environment. Consider the effect on your classroom of see-through clothing, lack of clothing, and extreme make-up or "clown-type" apparel.

Keep in mind that you are dealing with a very delicate situation. Court decisions concerning freedom of expression vary considerably but generally support reasonable rules and regulations. Acceptable dress varies from place to place, even in different buildings within the same district. Prior to the time Johnny shows up with his face painted with stripes or some other unusual appearance, you should have read district policies and talked with your principal to ensure that you understand what type of appearance is acceptable.

What do you do when one of these fads hits your classroom and causes great disruption? Well our friend Weatherspoon, has a simple straightforward solution - "get out".

As previously stated, understand what type of dress is acceptable within your school community. Discuss acceptable dress standards with your students. It then becomes your responsibility to determine when the appearance of a student is disruptive. You should work very closely with parents and administrators.

Above all, don't belittle or embarrass your students over this matter. Such action will ruin good student rapport. Try to understand and accept changing fads, unless, of course, they actually detract from the learning process. Remember, it is very important for students to dress in a manner similar to current styles.

After all, if you look at your old class yearbook, I'm sure you will be surprised at the similarity of you and your classmates. Be honest and admit how much you dress like your peers right now.

For all the rhetoric that we hear concerning the independence of young people today, they are still conforming creatures. They want, actually crave, peer acceptance, and will go to great lengths to obtain this approval. Therefore, try to ignore student appearance unless it is in direct violation of district policies, a safety factor, or disrupting the learning process.

SUMMARY OF SOLUTIONS

1. Be informed as to what is considered acceptable dress in your school.

2. Consult with administrators prior to confronting students.

3. To ensure consistency, administrators must make the final decision on student dress.

4. Set a good example for your students by always dressing in a proper and professional manner.

5. Remember, there is a relationship between respect and appearance.

6. Be prepared to adjust to changing times and styles.

7. Do not "put down" students' fads or styles unless it is an obvious violation of policies or disruptive to the learning process.

8. Don't encourage "dress up" or "dress down" days unless previously cleared with an administrator. Many teachers feel such activities are disruptive to the learning process.

Impulsive Behavior

Impulsive behavior can be defined as spontaneous reaction to situations without proper consideration of the consequences. This problem is not unique to the teaching profession. However, many of the classroom management problems discussed in this book stem from impulsive acts.

Consider the following examples of impulsive behavior by a teacher:

1. Striking or hitting a student

2. Sudden outburst of temper and swearing

3. Statements which cannot be supported such as "Never come back into my class"

4. Humiliating commands such as "Sit on the floor" or "Put the gum on your nose"

5. Stating opinions as if they were facts such as "You'll never get through college"

6. Name calling such as "You are stupid"

7. Jokes about political, racial, ethnic, social, or economic status

8. Accusations which cannot be supported by evidence.

As you can see, these actions are not planned. Often the consequences are unpleasant for everyone involved and generally the participants are sorry that the incident occurred. Your goal should be to avoid impulsive acts whenever possible.

One of the main goals of this entire book is to make educators aware of the more common problems confronting a classroom teacher. This awareness will allow you to anticipate potential conflicts and devise procedures which will eliminate or reduce the severity of the problem.

Don't assume that a particular incident will not occur. Everything and anything can and will occur at some time in a classroom. The wise teacher will plan a course of action for all eventualities.

When unexpected incidents occur, you can avoid impulsive decisions which may lead to a confrontation by the simple act of "buying some time". Delay making a final decision until you have had time to properly consider all ramifications. You can do this by quietly referring a student to the office for the remainder of the period. Above all, do not lose control of your temper and find some way to give yourself time to think about the situation at hand. It is also helpful to consult with a colleague or administrator before making your final decision.

Never place yourself in a situation where you say "I wish I hadn't said or done that" or "I never thought that would happen in my classroom."

SUMMARY OF SOLUTIONS

1. Make immediate decisions when situations involve student safety.

2. If safety is not involved, take action which does not require a final decision. For example "I'll see you after class" or "Report to the principal's office until further notice."

3. Avoid making rash decisions such as "You'll never get back in my class" or "I'll have you expelled from school."

4. Consult with administrators and colleagues before making major decisions.

5. Examine your discipline problems in retrospect. Ask yourself: "Is there something I could have done to prevent or reduce the severity of this problem? Did my behavior contribute to this problem?"

6. A calm and controlled reaction to most situations will reduce the severity of your problems.

7. In short, avoid placing yourself in "no win" situations.

Gum Chewing

"Young man, you can either put that gum on your nose or get out for the rest of the year," shouted Weatherspoon. Meanwhile, the students and teacher in the room next door are chewing gum. As you can see, an inconsistent policy such as this can easily lead to dissension among faculty members and student confusion. Educators throughout the country cannot agree on the effect of gum chewing on the learning process.

Educators who do not allow gum chewing argue that it deters from the learning process. They feel that it interferes with student recitation, and adds to classroom confusion when it ends up on desks, clothing, or hair.

Other teachers see nothing wrong with chewing gum and allow it in their classrooms. They argue that a gum chewing rule causes enforcement problems such as student alienation, punishment procedures, and results in a loss of teaching time. In other words, they feel that the problems of enforcing such a rule outweigh the negative aspects of chewing gum.

You must determine which approach to take. First, insure there are not building rules concerning gum chewing. If there are, follow the rules. If not, you should think through and explain your rules concerning gum in your class. For example:

1. Small amounts - so it doesn't interfere with proper speaking

2. No bubbles - keep it in your mouth

3. If it ends up on the floor, desks, or other improper places the guilty person will clean it up

4. If the mess continues, then no more gum in my room

Insure that your students understand your rules and the reason for them. Most students can handle chewing gum without causing problems. Treat them with respect and have high expectations and you'll get better results.

SUMMARY OF SOLUTIONS

1. Familiarize yourself with the official school policy regarding gum chewing.

2. Consult with fellow teachers.

3. If there is no official policy, formulate your own policy and procedures.

121

4. Make sure your classroom policies have the approval of your building administrator.

5. Explain your gum chewing policy to your classes. Because gum is highly controversial, punish only when the use of gum in your classroom is disruptive.

6. Chewing gum in a physical education class may be a safety factor.

Chapter XI
DISHONESTY

Cheating

Ever since the opening of the first school, some students have been looking for the easy way out - cheating. The definition of academic dishonesty varies, however it traditionally includes some or all of the following acts.

1. Copying another student's homework or test answers

2. Using "crib sheets" or "cheat notes" during tests

3. Having access to teacher answer sheets

4. Obtaining test questions from students who have already taken tests

5. Copying themes and other written papers from reference materials

6. Overuse of parental or older sibling assistance with homework or projects

7. Incorrect grading of assignments and tests in class

No attempt is made to list the multitude of ingenious and creative methods of cheating which students have invented.

Regardless of the method of cheating, the reason for cheating remains constant, that is, to enhance students' grades. Students should not rely on cheating since it is an irresponsible act which is socially unacceptable. Also, unless some action is taken to stop this practice it can become an epidemic. When grades are curved, honest students are penalized since all students are in effect competing with each other. Simply stated, the grades of honest students are lowered when cheating is allowed. As stated elsewhere in this text, cheating is but one of the many problems associated with grading. (See section on grading.)

This problem is easily dealt with by Weatherspoon. Our good fried tears up the test paper in front of the class. Weatherspoon was once reported to have said that by tearing up the paper and belittling the student in front of his peers the problem is solved.

There are better ways to handle students who write answers on hands or use some other method to cheat. First, you must recognize the possibility that some of "your children" will cheat. Remember, schools promote achievement and students desire to be successful. Sometimes students feel they must cheat to live up to the expectations of parents, peers, and teachers.

Prior to the first quiz have a talk with your students about cheating. Explain that when cheating takes place it destroys the grading curve and actually lowers the grades of honest students. Also, explain that you need to know if they are learning so you can gear assignments accordingly. Be sure to thoroughly explain your definition of cheating and the consequences for violating this rule. Therefore, cheating will not be tolerated. A statement of your expectations will do much to eliminate this problem. Most students will respond positively when they are well informed of your procedures.

You should develop standardized procedures to be followed during testing. These procedures should be designed to remove opportunities to cheat.

1. Ensure that all books and materials are on the floor or under the desk during testing

2. Seat students so it is more difficult to see another student's paper

3. Move around, stand behind students - do not sit at your desk

4. Ensure that students know exactly what to do after the test

5. Pick up test papers so students remain seated

6. Use different forms of the same test if you suspect cheating is taking place - color codes are effective

7. Read test questions out loud and make sure students thoroughly understand all questions before starting a test (This also helps poor readers.)

You will be confronted with two different types of problems regarding cheating. The first situation involves suspected or alleged cheating. Documentation and evidence are lacking. Be discreet in the manner in which you handle this situation. Never accuse and don't embarrass the student in front of the class. Conduct a private conference and offer the student the opportunity to take a different form of the same test. Oral questioning will also enable you to determine whether or not the student was adequately prepared. Above all, don't ignore suspected cases of cheating. However, showing concern without accusations or

124

punishment may be sufficient to deter similar situations in the future.

The other type of problem involves open and clear cases of cheating. There is no doubt that cheating has occurred and you must take some action. Ensure that your punishment is appropriate. Punishment should not exceed the value of a zero on that test or assignment. Don't assume that past or future work by this student involves cheating. Again, avoid open confrontations in front of the entire class. Conduct a private conference with the student. Chronic or severe cases may require referral to a counselor, administrator, or parent. (See section on parent conferences.)

Cheating may indicate other problems which you will want to examine. Possibly your academic requirements are too high for that student or even for the entire class. It could be that you're not sufficiently preparing your students. In other words, you need to change your method of teaching.

Listed below are a few suggestions which may help eliminate cheating or at least will give you a better understanding of the problem.

1. Failing a student or giving the grade of zero does not necessarily solve the problem

2. Ensure all students understand that those who allow copying are just as guilty as those who copy

3. Nearly all cheating can be eliminated by proper supervision

4. Homework assignments which can be easily copied should be avoided or receive a pass-fail grade

All too often in our society we hear "the only crime is getting caught". Ask yourself if this is really the way a classroom should function. Or are there other, more responsible, time tested values which you want students to understand and appreciate.

SUMMARY OF SOLUTIONS

1. Never accuse without proof.

2. Do not embarrass a student in front of peers.

3. Use alternative forms of the same test.

4. Conduct private conferences with students.

125

5. Involve administrators, counselors, and parents in chronic or severe cases.

6. Develop an organizational plan which will deter cheating. For example: All materials will be placed on the floor, use a seating arrangement which does not allow observing others.

7. Move around the room and supervise during tests.

8. Assignments or projects which can be easily copied should not be a major portion of the grade.

9. Use different colored pens when correcting papers in class.

10. Constantly review your expectations regarding cheating with your students.

11. Change your procedures occasionally and test your afternoon classes before your morning classes.

12. It is difficult to cheat on an essay question.

13. Cheating may indicate inappropriate class placement. A student may not be able to cope with the course work.

Classroom Security - Stealing

It appears that every society has a certain number of dishonest people. The public schools reflect society and this probably explains why stealing exists in schools. Educators have had to take action to cope with rising criminal and anti-social acts during the past two decades. In fact, one report states that theft in the public schools increased 117% from 1975-77.

This problem concerns classroom teachers for several reasons, not the least of which is the inconvenience it causes students and teachers. When small items like a projector bulb, a shop tool, or a meter stick are taken, it disrupts the education of entire classes.

Consider the impact on the educational system when some of these items are stolen:

1. Teacher's edition of the textbook

2. Grade book

3. Teacher's money or money collected for certain projects

4. Show and tell items

Frustration and suspicion are negative factors which are the direct result of classroom theft. Teachers become suspicious of students and students of their peers. This obviously detracts from a good learning climate. Replacement of stolen items can also be a serious problem if your budget is depleted. You may not be able to replace these items until new funds become available. By eliminating these devisive elements your classroom will be a more pleasant, positive, and productive room.

You should discuss all aspects of stealing with your students. Stress that theft will never be condoned no matter how minor the item involved. Also, you had better define theft. Some schools define theft as having in your possession something that belongs to someone else without their knowledge or permission. Never accept "I found it". Found items must be turned in immediately. Also, parents will be notified of all acts of stealing.

There are many things which you can do to curb theft. Don't tempt students. Keep materials locked up so they can't be easily removed. Establish procedures for checking out and checking in items prior to the bell. Use student assistance when feasible. This is especially important in shop or science classes.

Do not allow students to have free access to your desk. Let them know what your rules are regarding your personal and professional property. When money is collected, keep it in a money bag which is out of sight and stored in the vault.

What will you do if you discover that something of value disappears during class? You might consider not dismissing class and have a procedure so the guilty party can turn in the item without peer knowledge. For example, letting everybody look often turns up the "lost" object. If the item does not appear within a very short time, immediately obtain the assistance of an administrator.

Do not accuse a student of stealing in public. Even with certain proof, handle the situation in private. Then follow your school policy which will probably require restitution or some type of work program.

It is obvious that a problem of this magnitude cannot be completely eliminated by a classroom teacher. For example, the United States Office of Education report, "Violent Schools-Safe Schools" stated that twelve percent of secondary school teachers and eleven percent of secondary students have something worth more than one dollar stolen from them each month. Your awareness and use of the preceding suggestions can reduce the frequency and severity of this problem.

SUMMARY OF SOLUTIONS

1. Be aware of the fact that some of your students may be dishonest.

2. Define theft.

3. Establish check-in, check-out procedures for handling classroom materials.

4. Do not allow free or unsupervised access to your desk.

5. Materials not in use should be properly stored or locked in cabinets.

6. Develop a plan which you can use when personal or school property disappears during a class.

7. Encourage students to not bring unnecessary personal property to class or school.

8. Always lock your desk and room door when you are not in your classroom.

9. As with most problems, supervision will prevent most stealing.

10. Devote a few minutes at the end of each class period to check your room. Utilize student aides when possible.

11. Check your room after each class for materials left by students. Pick up such items and store in a safe place.

Classroom Vandalism

What is meant by classroom vandalism? Some examples are: writing on desks, scraping heels on the floor, gouging desks, writing in books, writing on walls and bulletin boards, and sticking gum on desks.

You may be asking yourself right now, "Why should I be concerned with these things? I'm a teacher not a policeman." Some educators believe and act in this manner. Everyone realizes your primary responsibility is the education of students. However, an appreciation and respect for other people's property is an essential part of anyone's education. Also, consider the monetary value of your classroom. It probably is comparable in value to an average home.

For several years Gallup has polled this nation asking what are the major concerns of people concerning education. Finance and vandalism have been near the top every year. Probably the most important reason for concerning yourself with preventing vandalism is that money spent to repair damage means your supply budget will suffer.

Weatherspoon has what many consider the easy, straightforward method to halt this problem. "If I catch you, I'll wrap you along-side your head with my pointer and send you to the principal." There are times when everyone would like to do this but prudent individuals don't. There are better ways to deal with this problem.

Why not explain classroom rules (as discussed elsewhere) and let students know you're proud of this room. Instilling a sense of pride and ownership in the classroom will help reduce the number of incidents. Remember, by simply expressing your concern, positive impact will be made upon most students.

The above suggestions will probably not completely eliminate the problem. You may still have a few students who continue to commit various acts of vandalism. What will you do? First, all students should have assigned desks and be required to sit in them. Chairs should be arranged so that no one sits too near a wall. In between classes check the desks. This will enable you to determine who has damaged a desk. When "Graffiti Melvin" writes on a desk tell him, "It wasn't written on when you came in and I think you should clean the desk." In fact, if he is a chronic offender he should probably wash all the desks in the room. If the desk is gouged or destroyed report the matter to your principal. The principal will determine the repair or replacement costs and insure that the student is held accountable. This procedure applies not only to desks but to all other forms of classroom vandalism.

It should be emphasized that simply moving around the classroom and being aware of what students are doing at all times is probably the best preventive technique a teacher can employ. Damage to text materials may be your greatest single area of classroom vandalism. Many educators advocate a system of assigning numbered materials to students. This includes books and items checked out for the entire year as well as items used only in the classroom. Students tend not to damage materials when they are held accountable for repair or replacement costs.

Invite the custodian to talk to your class. Have him explain that he tries to keep the school and room clean and attractive for students. When acts of vandalism occur it takes much time and effort to correct them. This is lost time and money. The custodian could obviously make better use of his time. The custodian also becomes more than a nameless face pushing a broom. He is a person and the students can identify with him and his problems.

Bulletin board damage can be reduced by involving students in their preparation. This saves you time and helps develop a sense of student pride in your room. Students often hesitate to damage the work of peers.

You may be thinking this all sounds good - but can you really stop vandalism? Take a tour of the classrooms in your building. You will observe quite a contrast. Some rooms are very attractive and display no signs of vandalism; while others are plain, unkept, and highly vandalized. Why the difference? Obviously the problem is not impossible to overcome. Some teachers have developed techniques which greatly reduce or eliminate classroom vandalism - so can you.

SUMMARY OF SOLUTIONS

1.   A positive attitude toward being responsible for the care and maintenance of the physical aspects of your classroom will go a long way toward eliminating classroom vandalism.

2.   Tell your students they are responsible for all materials and equipment assigned to them.

3.   Move around the room during class and be aware of student activity.

4.   Invite the custodian and principal into your room to explain the effect of vandalism on the total school program.

5.   Develop a sense of student pride in their classroom and school.

6. Establish a daily or weekly routine for checking desks, materials, and equipment.

7. Hold students accountable for all damage.

8. Involve students in contests to see which classrooms will have the least amount of vandalism over a given period of time.

9. Explain to your class what vandalism costs each year and how this money could be used in beneficial programs. Many students do not understand the cost of a new textbook or desk.

10. Vandalism usually occurs when students are angry, disinterested, inactive, and unsupervised.

Chapter XII
STUDENT AND TEACHER ATTITUDE

Positive Teacher Attitude

Most educators agree that learning is enhanced by enthusiastic teachers. This enthusiasm motivates and excites students. Much like a breeder reactor which feeds upon itself, students and other teachers find that a climate such as this is contagious.

Teachers should examine their attitudes and how other people perceive them. Do you give students the impression that you enjoy teaching? Do you like your students? Do you like teaching? These are types of questions that you should ask in order to determine your attitude toward teaching. Hopefully, you can answer yes. If not, learning will probably be diminished and discipline problems will increase.

Spend some time in the halls or observing other teachers. You will find that students talk to and seem to enjoy some teachers, while ignoring others. Why do students apparently dislike some teachers, act terrible and perform acts of vandalism in their classrooms?

Weatherspoon was asked this question and had a simple, ready answer, "Students are poorly disciplined, won't work, and don't respect adults." Weatherspoon may be right, but most classes are really enjoyable. Students seem to like and enjoy school They willingly do their work and are not disruptive. Why the disparity? You will find at least part of the answer when you examine teacher attitude.

Teaching is not a popularity contest. However, if you get along with your students, you'll experience fewer discipline problems and students will learn more and work harder. In short, a positive attitude will help you be a more effective teacher and at the same time your job will be much easier.

Take a good look at how you treat students. Do you smile at them? Do you speak to them in the halls? Do you try an occasional joke? Even if unsuccessful, students will appreciate your trying. If you don't do these things, maybe you have a negative attitude. There are some don'ts that go hand in glove with the above do's.

1. Don't use sarcasm and cynicism

2. Don't embarrass students in front of their peers

3. Don't talk down to students and their parents

4. Don't openly criticize the educational program

You are urged to treat all students with respect. Be polite, it won't hurt and will make you a better person.

Schools needs teachers who are self confident; teachers who are good actors; teachers who can appear enthused about everything they teach; and finally teachers who can leave their personal problems at home. Studies concerned with the influence of teacher behavior upon student actions suggest that what the teacher says and does in class has a direct influence on the type of student behavior exhibited. 1/

SUMMARY OF SOLUTIONS

1. Examine your attitudes toward students, school, other educators, and perhaps yourself.

2. Based on the above, determine whether you have a positive or negative attitude toward your position as a teacher.

3. A negative attitude will make it very difficult to establish rapport or respect with students and fellow educators.

4. A positive attitude will probably result in a healthy self concept and success as an educator.

5. Try to go through an entire work day without criticizing anyone or anything. Keep score of your efforts.

6. Observe other staff members in terms of general attitudes toward students and teaching. Try to see yourself in proper perspective.

7. When things go wrong, we have three choices:
    a. Gripe about it
    b. Blame someone else
    c. Try a positive and constructive solution
    We really don't need to practice the first two.

1/ National Association of Secondary School Principals Bulletin, 60:65-69 Nov., 1976.

Students Not Working

All too often teachers are faced with the problem of a student who won't work. For those of you still in college, not working may be incomprehensible. However, experienced teachers often report that students not working is a severe problem. School discipline records substantiate these reports since a large number of students are annually referred to the office for not working.

Why is this a problem for the classroom teacher? Students who are not working usually disrupt the learning process. Besides, even if a student is not disruptive, teachers still have a professional obligation to instruct each and every student in their classroom.

It is possible that some students really don't care if they pass or fail. However, there usually is a reason for lack of effort. Weatherspoon never considered finding out why students aren't working, they are just failed. It is assumed you will make every effort to determine why a student isn't working. You should examine possible problems which prevent students from achieving and consider corrective steps.

As with many other problems, the first step should be a private conference with the student. Simply ask, why are you not working? It could be that the family just doesn't have the money to purchase paper, pencils, and other paraphernalia. In this case, contact your school administrator concerning procedures for dealing with indigent students.

Physical problems such as poor eyesight, hearing problems, or improper nutrition may also prevent students from taking part in classroom activities. One of the author's children experienced a physical need in third grade. She needed glasses badly. She had always been an excellent student and the parents just weren't aware of her need. If this problem had gone untended she could have developed a serious learning problem.

Another reason why students sometimes do not attempt school work is fear of failure. "To try is to fail" is a phrase ever present in the minds of many students. Everyone likes to do things which allow success. We all need success! That is the way fear of failure is overcome. You are the vital link. Give assignments which insure success. Soon you will find students are ready and willing to try tasks that are more difficult. They believe in you and much more importantly, they believe in themselves.

Examine assignments and their relationship to non-working students. Let the class know what you expect them to do and learn prior to giving assignments. This will allow each student to plan just how much time to devote to assignments. Insure that your assignments are high quality and not just busy work. All too often assignments look and sound great but really are rather shallow. Your assignments should be meaningful, conform to the objectives of the lesson, and relate to the real world.

Ask yourself if it is practical or even possible for all students to do the same assignment. The first step toward individualizing instruction is to identify needs and interests of each student. Personalizing each student's assignment will help motivate students. Remember, lack of motivation is a primary reason for "not working". Many educators feel that you can't force students to learn.

Weatherspoon often uses the excuse for irrelevant subject matter or poorly prepared lesson plans that it is in the curriculum guide or the administration requires me to teach this way. This excuse is unacceptable.

Another procedure is referred to as the "little red school house" philosophy. If you don't do your work, you'll stay in at recess (if you have one), at noon, or after school until you finish your work. This method should be used only with truly lazy students. Those students who have physical, social, or learning problems would be punished for something beyond their control.

After trying several of the techniques mentioned above you may still have a few students that do not do their work. These students should be referred to the guidance office for extensive testing to determine causes of behavior and to suggest further steps to correct the problem. You may also wish to discuss the problem with other teachers and administrators who are familiar with the student.

Teachers don't want students to get the idea that they can get away with not working. This attitude could infect the entire class. If all else fails, the student may have to be removed from the room. Remember, not working may become a form of covert defiance (see defiance).

Some teachers feel that students have the right to fail. Ask yourself if you really believe this. Are you sure students have the right to make this choice? Do you have the right to allow them to fail?

You - not the administration or anyone else - must determine the policy and establish priorities for your classroom. You must decide if your students will fail or be successful.

SUMMARY OF SOLUTIONS

1. Make every effort to determine why some students don't work.

2. Be excited about your subject and motivate students to want to work and learn.

3. Impress upon students the importance of doing their work.

4. Conduct a private conference.

5. Assignments should allow all students some measure of success.

6. Check with other teachers to find out how they deal with certain students.

7. Are you assigning too much work?

8. Do you grade and return all assignments punctually?

9. Are your assignments clear and well understood by your students.

10. Relate your required work to the interests of students.

11. Examine your teaching techniques:
    a. How much class time is devoted to seat work - worksheets, etc.?
    b. How much class time is devoted to interaction between teacher and students?
    Some teachers over do seat work and students simply "burn out". Try other methods of learning lessons that do not involve worksheets.

12. Students may not be working because the teacher is not working hard enough to motivate the students.

It is unfortunate, but many schools have a Weatherspoon on their staff. As noted in previous sections, this person typifies the negative teacher who dislikes students, is unhappy, inflexible, and generally unpleasant.

Examine some of the characteristics of teachers who have negative attitudes. These individuals usually openly complain about students whom they feel are disruptive, do not work and get low grades, or are not academically prepared to take their class.

Weatherspoons often blame other teachers for inadequately preparing students. Negative teachers also complain that their colleagues run loose classes, are overly friendly with students, have low standards, give high grades, and in other words cater to the students.

Administrators also feel the wrath of negative teachers who feel they are not supported in terms of discipline, salaries, budget, and general working conditions. Parents are also the objects of complaints and are accused of not being cooperative or supportive of teachers.

The list of examples of teacher negativism could go on indefinitely. However, suffice to say, these people have job related problems. These problems might be that they simply do not like teaching, their grade level, or the subject matter taught. These individuals often have severe interpersonal problems not only at work but in all aspects of their life.

The negative attitudes described above have an adverse effect on the educational process and climate of an entire school building. Constant griping and complaining lowers the morale of other staff members and students. This in turn may diminish the efforts of students and other teachers. Productivity in the form of student achievement generally declines in such situations. An accepted fact is, unless you are excited and highly motivated about teaching, achievement will suffer.

The first step in solving teacher negativism is to personally recognize and admit that the problem exists. However, it is difficult for most people to personally recognize their own shortcomings. Therefore, it is suggested that all teachers go through periodic self evaluation. Listen to constructive comments from students, peers, and administrators. Keep an open mind!

If you determine that you are developing negative feelings toward your job, it is necessary that you consider corrective action. Consider the following:

1. Change grade level and/or subject

2. Consider a sabbatical or leave of absence

3. Change your methods of teaching

4. Develop and implement new classroom management techniques

5. Associate with good teachers who have positive attitudes

6. Personal problems may require professional counseling

7. Ask your building administrator for assistance - a simple change in your schedule or room assignment may help

8. Avoid negative conversations

9. Visit classes of enthusiastic teachers

10. The poor job market for teachers has literally prevented "change". Lack of change leads to stagnation and burnout. Be innovative enough to find a way of changing when it becomes apparent that negativism is becoming a part of your life.

In general, some sort of "change" usually enhances or promotes positive attitudes and your outlook on life. This will not only improve your performance at school but will also help you cope with personal and family problems.

SUMMARY OF SOLUTIONS

1. See list above.

Keeping Your Perspective

One definition of perspective is the power to see or think of things in their true relationship to each other. If you allow things to get out of perspective it will affect the decisions you make. This may adversely affect your relationships with students and colleagues.

It is especially difficult to keep things in perspective if you are tired, upset, ill, or short on patience. Perspective is often associated with the time of year. For example, you probably will have fewer problems in September than you do in March. Teacher stress and burnout tend to increase in the latter part of the school year.

Some specific problems which may arise are:

1. Frequent loss of temper

2. Impulsive decisions

3. Overly severe disciplinary action

4. Excessive complaining

5. Disagreements and arguments

6. Categorizing students as all bad, lazy, or dumb

7. Raising your voice

As can be seen, loss of perspective will create many problems which otherwise could have been avoided.

So, how can you avoid these situations and keep the proper perspective throughout the school year. Personal awareness is a major step. Just knowing the possibility exists for these incidents to occur will help avoid them.

Specifically, try to avoid negative conversations. They tend to reinforce the exact things you are trying to avoid. For instance, walk into the faculty lounge and say, "Let's talk about all the good things that have happened this week."

There are many other steps which will help you avoid problems with perspective:

1. Associate with exciting and positive people

2. Think about your better students

3. Change your teaching style

4. Change your daily routine. Trade teaching positions with someone in your building or district for one or two days

5. Rest and relaxation

6. Get involved in non-school activities

7. Give time and patience a chance

8. Try a joke or laugh at your perceived problems

Many of these problems may disappear overnight.

Make every effort to separate your job from your personal problems. For example, salary negotiations in the spring should have nothing to do with your relationship with students or administrators. Remember, perspective is the ability to discriminate and prioritize.

Everyone must be reminded of the true and original purpose of schools, which is to educate children.

SUMMARY OF SOLUTIONS

1. Refer to the items listed above

A little praise does
wonders for one's sense of hearing

Chapter XIII
SOCIAL AND PERSONAL PROBLEMS

Cliques, Groups, and Gangs

Most students tend to be very gregarious. They associate with other students who have similar values, goals, and aspirations. For example, most schools have well identified groups such as the "soches," "jocks," "hoods," "eggheads," and "drug users." Each group can be identified by either dress, behavior, or particular speech patterns. Unfortunately, groups may cause problems for classroom teachers.

The values of certain groups prohibit them from being cooperative in the classroom. They may challenge classroom rules and procedures. As you can see, behavior such as this is disruptive. Other groups may not be as difficult, but can be equally disruptive. Differences between groups can also lead to problems. These clashes can vary from petty bickering, to not speaking, or to outright violence.

Your first task is to become aware of the existence of groups, their membership, and the nature of the differences among the groups in your school. Let your students know early in the year that you are aware of individual differences and the various groups with which they associate. Emphasize that you will not tolerate disruptive behavior because of these differences. Be very careful to treat student groups equally and fairly. Don't put yourself in the position where you can be accused of favoritism to any student group.

Teachers should make every attempt to understand all students. You must respect differences in dress, looks, ways of talking, likes and dislikes. Don't make derogatory remarks about any group. Don't criticize things that are important to students. If you alienate students, your effectiveness as a teacher is greatly diminished.

The right or wrong combination of students can literally destroy the learning process. They can, and will, ask dumb questions; constantly ask to use the bathroom; or concoct other reasons to avoid working. These same individuals may be model students when isolated from others in their clique.

Work with the building administrator and/or guidance office to change the schedule or room of one or more of your students. If you can't get part of the clique moved to another class, then in-room corrective action must take place.

Students in disruptive groups must be separated. Move a member of the clique so that eye contact with other members will be most difficult. Students with close personal relationships need not be near each other to plan disruptive activities.

Another problem often caused by cliques is "picking" on students outside of their group. If left unchecked they can make life miserable for other students. Certain value clarification activities or role playing techniques may help these students understand how unpleasant life is for those students being harassed.

Another bit of advice - don't think you're the only teacher having problems with cliques or groups. Talk with other teachers and see if they have developed techniques that work. Remember, belonging to a group is part of the American way of life. Keep in perspective your duties as a teacher. You will not change or eliminate groups which you view with disfavor. By belittling cliques you will only alienate yourself from large groups of students.

SUMMARY OF SOLUTIONS

1. Become aware of the various student groups in your school. Know their values and differences.

2. Tell your students that you are aware of groups but you will not tolerate any problems associated with different cliques.

3. Do not criticize or praise specific groups. In other words, stay neutral.

4. If cliques become disruptive, investigate the possibilities of schedule changes.

5. Physically separate group members within your classroom.

6. Talk with other teachers and share successful techniques for dealing with disruptive groups.

7. Teach students to respect individual and group differences.

8. Be aware that types and values of groups in our schools do change with time. Don't become buried in the past. Keep up with the times as it may help you prevent problems.

Social, Economic and Cultural Differences

Secondary teachers normally teach five or six different classes each day. This could represent 150-200 students. Another way of looking at this is to think of these students as representing an equal number of families. In a heterogeneous community, these students and families would probably exhibit considerable differences in social, economic, and cultural lifestyles.

Problems arise when teachers do not recognize or are unable to cope with the differences mentioned above. Many educators have "tunnel vision" partly due to their academic background and unawareness of the diversity of the community in which they are teaching. As a result, whether intentionally or unintentionally, teachers often try to impose their values on students.

Alienation often results from this clash of values among educators, students and parents. The learning process is obviously affected due to poor rapport, lack of harmony, trust and respect. Lack of respect for individual differences will probably result in classroom disruption. Subtle things often tell some students that they are not valued as much as their more favored classmates. Imagine what this does to the self image of these students. Little wonder that they become alienated and develop into discipline problems.

Teachers need to understand what is generally acceptable behavior in the homes of all students. What are the goals and aspirations of parents and students? With this information you can plan lessons which will relate to the majority of students.

You must also be aware that some students cannot afford expensive supplies and clothing. If these items are praised, you are telling students they are not as good as others because of economic status.

Accept and understand differences such as morals, traits, dress, speech and food. By respecting these differences you will get along better with students and parents. You may also wish to review the section on getting to know your students.

SUMMARY OF SOLUTIONS

1. Become aware of the social, economic, and cultural differences that exist among students in your classes and community.

2. Respect these differences and remain neutral.

3. Be careful not to make disparaging remarks.

145

4. Plan lessons which are commensurate with the social, economic, and cultural level of your students.

5. Remember, you must have rapport with and the respect of your students to teach effectively.

Alcohol and Drugs

A sad but true fact is that some students do indulge in alcohol and drugs. It is to your advantage to be cognizant of the fact that even elementary students may come to school "high" at some time. Some surveys indicate that a number of secondary students arrive at school under the influence for the first period of the day, this percentage increases after lunch.

Drugs and alcohol affect students in a variety of negative ways. In some cases, students become lackadaisical and drowsy, while others may become violent and defiant. This is a problem for classroom teachers because drugs and alcohol affect student achievement and behavior which may disrupt an entire class. You should also be aware of the fact that a student under the influence of drugs or alcohol may pose a safety factor to himself, other students, and educators.

Weatherspoon may ignore the problem or just toss the offender out of the room. Most teachers can't be this callous and whenever possible provide help for the student.

First, be alert for deviant behavior. The use of controlled substances often affects the general attitude and personality of the user. As an example, a very studious and happy student may suddenly develop a sullen personality and a "don't care" attitude toward school work. You should make every attempt to find out why these changes have taken place.

Some types of alcohol and drugs emit distinct and easily identifiable odors. Your local police department, administration or social service agency will assist you in becoming familiar with the identification of students who are under the influence.

If your school has a written policy regarding substance abuse, be sure to read it, understand it, and follow it. In the absence of a written policy, confer with your building administrator.

You probably will want to handle these cases with great care and discretion. Do not openly accuse or confront suspected students in the presence of their peers. It is probably best to quietly invite the student into the hall and escort him to the nurse or principal. Do not send the student to either destination unescorted.

Individuals in this condition may be a danger to themselves or others. Regardless of the situation, it is suggested that you immediately inform the school nurse or administrator of your suspicions. This can be accomplished by sending a student to the office with a sealed note. Administrators will investigate and handle the situation.

Be cognizant that student behavior is affected by many factors other then drugs or alcohol. For example, school activities, successes, failures, student's personal and social life all have a drastic affect on observable behavior. Do not make the mistake of assuming that students are under the influence of drugs until you have adequate proof. Above all, discuss suspected drug use only with those in authority and never in a social setting.

Drug and alcohol use is a major problem throughout our society. Because students are an integral part of this society, you must anticipate the possibility that this problem may find its way into your school and classroom. You should be ready and able to adequately handle these situations should they occur.

SUMMARY OF SOLUTIONS

1. Be alert for deviant behavior and strange smells.

2. Unusually frequent requests for locker or restroom passes may indicate a problem.

3. Sudden changes in attitude toward school may indicate a problem.

4. Confer with administrators, counselors, and nurses regarding suspicions.

5. Know and follow your school policy regarding alcohol and drugs.

6. Do not openly accuse or confront suspected students without hard evidence.

7. Administrators should make all final decisions regarding drug and alcohol abuse.

8. It is most difficult to prove the use of many drugs. Be patient and refer students with problems to the guidance department.

Student Cleanliness

As stated in other sections, your students may be a very heterogeneous group. Therefore, the attitudes and values regarding personal appearance and cleanliness will vary. Some students will come to school wearing very dirty or unkept clothing. Others may exhibit obviously dirty hands, face, or hair. Odors may accompany this general lack of cleanliness.

You will experience classroom problems as a result of student uncleanliness. For example, some students may refuse to associate or sit near a student who is unwashed or is wearing dirty clothing. Consider the problems associated with a comment such as the following, "I'm not going to sit next to him. He stinks." This type of situation is very embarrassing, may lead to further harassment, and obviously disrupts the learning process.

Weatherspoon probably would say, "You're right, he stinks. Get out until you're cleaned up." But really, is this a proper, decent or humane way to handle this problem?

Students have cleanliness problems for many and sundry reasons. Too long between baths or showers, unwashed clothes, or the meunstrual period are a few reasons for the problem. Because of environmental and/or physical changes, many students may be unaware of their physical appearance.

How will you handle the student who, in fact, does smell? It really isn't fair to others to be forced to sit by this source of odor, yet the student has feelings as does everyone. Make every attempt to get through the period by taking no obvious action. You might state that it appears you're not feeling well, would you like to go to the nurse or office? Do this quietly and discreetly. The student may come from an unclean home. Unless you have excellent rapport with the student, you may wish to refer him to another person such as the counselor or school nurse. Remember, whatever happens you're going to have to maintain some type of relationship with the student and parents.

What about dirty clothes? This may be the result of negligence within the student's home or it may be an economic problem. A social worker or nurse should make this determination.

Some service organizations will purchase a complete suit of clothes for students. Many schools also budget money for indigent students. But this action should be taken only after consultation with the principal and parents. Remember, many parents would have hurt feelings if this action were taken without their consent. In the case of parental neglect, the administration is faced with a delicate parental counseling situation.

A problem that is more prevalent in the lower grades but occasionally crops up in secondary schools is when someone has an accident, that is, they didn't get to the bathroom in time. How can you save the student from even more embarrassment? If you decide the student cannot go to the washroom to clean himself, then send a trusted student for a nurse, counselor, administrator, or other educator. Upon their arrival, immediately get your class out of the room. Library work often fits into the lesson plan during such emergencies.

Throughout your handling of matters such as these it is extremely important to remember that if you handle them in a discreet professional manner, students will respect you.

If you blunder and unduly hurt feelings and embarrass students, you'll be thought of as an insensitive teacher. The choice is yours. We know you'll prefer the former.

SUMMARY OF SOLUTIONS

1. Handle all cases of student cleanliness with utmost discretion and diplomacy.

2. Refer cleanliness problems to the school nurse or social worker before they become a crisis.

3. The physical education department can be helpful by requiring showers.

4. Clothing can be purchased for indigent students.

5. Never openly criticize or discuss such problems in your classroom.

6. A good class rule is "We never make comments about other people which could hurt their feelings."

7. Student cleanliness and appearance may be a form of parental neglect or abuse. Report your concerns to the proper school authorities.

Chapter XIV
PUNISHMENT

Corporal Punishment

Whatever your views concerning corporal punishment you should know that its legality is being upheld by the courts. But only when administered under certain prescribed conditions in the school office - not by an angry classroom teacher. Simply stated, you may anticipate problems if you inflict physical pain on a student in the classroom. Actions such as slapping, pinching, shaking, kicking, or similar methods of physical discipline are generally unacceptable. Your problem will not only be an angry parent and alienated student, but you will be in flagrant violation of school board rules. Therefore, the building administrator may be unable to support you and may be forced to take disciplinary action against you. Plainly stated, it is advised that you never touch a student for disciplinary reasons.

However, teachers will occasionally lose their tempers and strike or slap a student. It does happen and you need to think about it now. What will you do if you slap or hit a student?

Notify the principal immediately. Tell the details truthfully. This is not a time to procrastinate or tell half truths. Talk to the student after class, at noon or after school. Be big enough to admit that your temper got the best of you. Call the parents, explain what happened and what led up to the incident. Admit you made a mistake. Most parents will not take you to court - especially when you instigate a show of concern over the incident.

One of the authors once called a parent concerning a slapping incident. After listening to the entire explanation, the parent asked, "Did he settle down and get to work?" When told yes, the parent said, "Good, thanks for calling."

The authors are opposed to manhandling students. When you feel yourself getting very angry at a student, have him sit in the hall or sent to the office for the rest of the period. This allows for a cooling off period which enables you to handle the situation in a rational manner.

Remember, it is much easier to prevent problems than to correct an ugly incident.

SUMMARY OF SOLUTIONS

1. Generally, teachers are not allowed to administer corporal punishment in a classroom.

2. As a general rule, never touch a student in anger.

3. If you make the mistake of physically disciplining a student, notify the building administrator immediately, call the parents, and conduct a private conference with the student.

4. Make sure you know your building rules and district policies regarding corporal punishment. This is an area where you can get into legal difficulties in a hurry.

Other Forms of Punishment

This text is dedicated to the principles of classroom management. As stated in the introduction, the authors believe when teachers develop and implement classroom management procedures, disruptive acts will be greatly reduced or eliminated. However, educators know that perfect classroom management has not been achieved in all schools by all teachers.

When classroom management does not exist, breaks down, or doesn't work you end up with what is commonly called "discipline problems". These conditions exist for several reasons:

1. Many colleges of education do not adequately deal with the realities of classroom life. Beginning teachers are often shocked at their classroom problems. They complain that their education did not prepare them to either anticipate or solve the multitude of classroom management problems with which they are confronted. This results in discipline problems.

2. Some teachers do not believe in classroom management or at the very least, do not practice it. This results in discipline problems.

3. Some teachers do not appear to have good teaching skills or the right kind of "teaching personality". This also results in discipline problems.

4. Finally, some of the blame must rest with the students. Although the authors firmly believe most students will respond to positive classroom management procedures, a few students do not. This results in discipline problems.

Regardless of the reasons, poor classroom management results in an increase in discipline problems. However, even outstanding teachers with excellent classroom management skills will occasionally have discipline problems. So, what happens next?

The educational society practically demands that poor behavior be punished in some manner. Punishment may be defined as supplying an aversive such as: pain, fear, anxiety, frustration, humiliation, boredom, embarrassment or physical discomfort. In any event, punishment is enforced obedience. It is intended to make a student behave in order to avoid something unpleasant. It's an attempt to correct a problem after the act has been committed. This could easily be called retribution but it is intended to be reformatory in nature. Some punishments are designed to be protective of other students in that offenders are isolated or removed from the mainstream of the classroom. The authors hope all punishment is designed for the purpose of behavior modification. Unfortunately, some forms of punishment are counter-productive and may create more problems than they solve.

Consider the following list of punishments which usually result in confrontations and "no win" situations for teachers:

1. Physical contact such as grabbing, shaking, or hitting

2. Shouting and screaming

3. The use of obscene language and calling students names

4. Highly embarrassing commands such as "put the gum on your nose" or "sit on the floor"

5. Lowering academic grades for disciplinary reasons

6. Assigning extra homework or tests as punishment

7. Personal and negative references and comparisons to other family members

8. Threats that can't be carried out

9. Forced apologies

10. Removal of lunchroom privileges

11. Keeping entire class in after school

12. Public ridicule of any kind

All of the above acts generally result in student and/or parental alienation. They may be in violation of school policy which will place your administrator in a position where he cannot be supportive. Acts such as these should be avoided.

There are other forms of classroom punishment which are in a "gray area". In other words, depending upon the teacher and student involved, an action may or may not be productive. These actions are further affected by catalysts such as: teacher personality, rapport with students, sex, type of class or community. Some examples of these actions are:

1. Copying pages of books or writing sentences

2. Sitting in a corner

3. Taking items away from students

154

4. Use of sarcasm

5. Intimidation or "put downs"

6. Changing seats

7. Isolation

8. Restriction of privileges

9. Referrals to the office

10. Teacher detention

11. Sit in the hall

12. Behavior contracts

Any of the above actions may be successful or unsuccessful depending on how they are handled. For example, changing seats may result in student defiance if this change results in a situation which is highly embarrassing to the student.

Over the years, other forms of punishment have generally been found to be productive. Again, caution must be exercised. For example, requiring a student to come in after class usually is beneficial since it results in a student-teacher conference. However, if this results in an athlete missing a football game, it could become disastrous. Work details such as washing writing off desks seems fitting because the punishment relates to the violation.

As stated in another section, record keeping procedures which require students to sign a notebook for minor infractions has proven highly successful. Parental telephone calls and/or conferences are also very productive if handled in a positive manner.

As stated throughout this text, the critical aspect of management or punishment is the promulgation of your classroom rules, procedures, and general expectations. Students generally respond in a positive manner if they fully understand rules, why rules are needed, and the consequences of breaking these rules.

SUMMARY OF SOLUTIONS

1. Some forms of punishment are counter-productive and cause more problems than they solve.

2. Ensure that punishment always "fits the crime".

3. Use positive forms of punishment.

4. Discuss punishment possibilities with students prior to making a final decision.

5. Be careful not to use threats which cannot be implemented.

6. Avoid punishments which are related to school work such as writing or lowering academic grades.

7. If not in conflict with school policy, issue a separate conduct grade which is based on objective data. (See section on record keeping)

8. Use punishment to positively change poor behavior. Do not use punishment as an act of vengeance.

9. Use rewards to achieve proper behavior.

10. Try preventive classroom management techniques prior to resorting to punishment. Punishment is not the final cure for a problem.

Referrals to the Principal's Office

The principal's office exists for the sole reason of providing support services to staff and students in the building. It is not the purpose of this section to deter you from sending behavior problems to the school office. However, you should be aware of some potential pitfalls inherent in the referral process.

You know the story about the little boy who cried "wolf" so often that when he needed help no one listened. Unfortunately, this situation may apply to the relationship between the classroom teacher and the school administrator. Teachers may overuse the referral process to the point where it becomes ineffective. In these cases, the teacher may also lose the respect of students, peers, and administrators.

The exact opposite of the above situation occurs when a teacher never sends a student to the office. This is satisfactory assuming good classroom management techniques are in effect and the teacher is in control of the classroom. However, failure to refer students is counter-productive if the students are out of control. In this case, a teacher is not utilizing what can be a very effective disciplinary technique.

Another problem is a situation where a teacher continually threatens to send students to the office but never follows through. This teacher will soon have serious problems when students realize the threats are meaningless.

As can be seen from the above discussion, referrals to the office may or may not be productive. Effective referrals depend upon many factors. For example, do not make referrals based on information or incidents which you have not personally observed. If you accuse a student unjustly, it may result in permanent alienation or loss of student/teacher rapport.

When you send a student to the office always send along some form of communication. Ensure that your note explains accurately what happened and action you expect. Remember, students may lie. If your note isn't accurate, the principal may take some action which will compound the problem. Always check to ensure that the student reported to the office.

An even more effective referral procedure is to take the student personally to the office. Ask to see the principal privately, then explain what happened in a calm manner. Always allow the student to state his position while you are still present. A note of caution, make sure someone, like the teacher next door, is supervising your class.

Solving the problems of disruptive students is even more effective. Consider the possibility of a teacher/student/principal conference where all parties can have a calm and candid discussion. No punitive action is taken as a result of such a conference. This simple procedure solves many little problems before they develop into major confrontations.

Keep in mind that the principal's office will probably not view the problem child in the exact manner which you do. Exercises in classroom management classes have indicated that groups of teachers and administrators will differ on how they would handle the same referral. A referral indicates your willingness to accept another person's help.

When should you send a disruptive student to the office? There are certain situations which always warrant sending a pupil to the office such as use of obscenity in the classroom, physical assault, or outright acts of defiance. Less severe offenses should be handled by the teacher. After you have tried several techniques described in other sections of this book, by all means look to the office for help and support.

SUMMARY OF SOLUTIONS

1. Be consistent in the use of office referrals.

2. Office referrals do not indicate teacher failure, but can be an effective disciplinary technique.

3. Make sure that you accurately communicate the reason for the referral to the office.

4. Always check with the office to ensure that the referred student arrived.

5. A good preventive technique is to conduct a conference with the student, teacher, and principal.

6. Document referrals with objective data.

7. Never refer on the basis of suspicion.

8. Students must thoroughly understand why they are being referred to the office.

9. Your classroom rules should be clear to everyone as to when and for what reason a student will be sent to the office.

10. Work in the school office and handle a few referrals to help get a perspective of the problem.

11. Supply the principal with a copy of your classroom discipline procedures. It is important that the principal understands what actions have preceded the referral.

12. Large numbers of referrals may indicate a need for help in the area of classroom management.

13. Documentation of student misbehavior is invaluable information on a referral form.

Chapter XV
SEVERELY HANDICAPPED STUDENTS

Hyperactive Kids

Excessive restlessness, nervousness, clicking pens, shuffling feet, or constant squirming are examples of common classroom problems. This type of behavior is called hyperactivity.

One important point to keep in mind is that students differ in their ability to sit reasonably quiet for varying lengths of time. Keep in mind that restlessness is normal with young people. Students must move - they really have growing pains. Be aware of this and take it into account in your planning. Some students have severe physiological problems which make it difficult for them to take part in normal classroom activities. These more serious problems are usually diagnosed by medical doctors and medication is often prescribed.

Hyperactivity seems to bother teachers more than students. Students are used to distractions. Most adults cannot comprehend how students can study in the presence of loud music, television, and interrupting phone calls. Most students successfully complete school assignments in spite of these apparent distractions.

Before you take action to solve apparent hyperactivity problems in the classroom, be sure they are problems. Does the activity disrupt the learning situation or does it "bother" you? If you determine it is a detriment to the learning process, then you should take corrective action.

It is often said that the best defense is a good offense and our good friend Weatherspoon has a great offense. Use the yardstick often and with great force. However, there is no research to indicate that a spanking can change a basic physiological condition.

If pure punishment will not correct distractions caused by excessive activity, then what techniques can a teacher employ. Plan classroom activities so that students have the opportunity to move and not become restless. It helps to have at least three different types of learning activities each period. This should allow for some movement and keep interest levels high.

After identifying students with the most severe problems, use them as helpers. Let them pass out papers and books, make trips to the office or takes notes to their destination. This activity helps students burn off excess energy.

For students with less severe problems, consider having a "carpet corner" with pillows. A hyperactive student can sit

161

there, squirm, and still take part in class activities. You might also consider obtaining some bean bag chairs. Use school funds or let students bring them from home. Whoever said one must sit at a regular desk to learn anyway?

Talk privately with hyperactive students. Let them know you understand their need for movement. Work out an understanding whereby students let you know when their capacity for being quiet has been reached. Have a plan which allows student participation in some worthwhile activity which will solve both your problems. Remember, a good teacher will take care of individual needs while not detracting from the needs of the entire class.

All of these suggestions will help burn up energy and solve the restlessness problem. A side benefit is that this will enhance your rapport with students and therefore they may study and work harder in your class.

If all of these suggestions fail you might consider putting a chair in the hall. When hyperactivity gets out of hand have the student to sit outside. Leave the door open so you can continue supervision and allow the student to hear what is happening in the room. It may be necessary to talk to the principal. Explain that you need some help but really don't want Mr. Squirm punished. Maybe a special room can be established so students can move around, or just allow the student to spend some time in the office. Another idea that has worked is to ask your principal or counselor to arrange for extra time in physical education.

Remember that unless the squirming and moving really disrupts the learning process, just overlook it if at all possible.

SUMMARY OF SOLUTIONS

1. Overlook hyperactivity unless it distracts other students.

2. Conduct a private student/teacher conference. Make sure that the student is aware of his problem and that you will try to be understanding.

3. Require your students to personally keep a record of the number of times they distract class.

4. Use hyperactive students as aides.

5. Lesson plans should allow for varied activities with some movement.

6. Establish a corner of the classroom for excessively active students.

7. Seat hyperactive students in the periphery of your vision.

8. Don't forget that a certain amount of restlessness is normal for young people.

9. Review the physiological and psychological characteristics of the age group you are teaching. Student behavior may or may not be normal and it will help you get your perspective.

Mentally Disturbed Students

Schools are a reflection of our society. Therefore, you should expect to encounter similar extremes of individuals in schools as are found in the non-school world. Remember, this outside of school culture contains mental health centers, mental hospitals, prisons, and a very large number of psychologists and psychiatrists. It is a little wonder that a certain percentage of mentally ill students are in classrooms. Furthermore, Public Law 94-142 states that all students are entitled to an education. Even though there are special classes for these students, you must first be able to identify them. Failure to do so may cause serious problems.

If you do not know which students have mental problems, you may mishandle certain situations which then become explosive and extremely disruptive to your classroom. The solution is to be informed about special cases ahead of time. However, it is not always possible to "know" ahead of time. This is especially true with new students with no school records. In these cases, you must be aware of identification procedures.

Some symptoms of mental instability are:

1. A behavior that has a peculiar compulsive or driven quality - these students really don't know why they act as they do

2. Soliciting punishment - students does the very thing he knows will result in punishment

3. Behavior that is accompanied by inappropriately intense emotions - becoming murderous during a fight, screaming out of control, kicking or injuring oneself

4. Behavior not characteristic of age - student who is fifteen acting like a six year old

5. Behavior followed by intense remorse of short duration - this is then followed by additional offenses and more intense remorse

When you observe deviant behavior such as suggested above:

1. Record accurate accounts of behavior

2. Refer the problem to the school psychologist

3. Conduct a parental conference involving teachers, administrators, counselors and psychologists

4. Don't label the student - let specialists advise you of particulars

5. Map out a plan of action

Dealing with mentally disturbed students can be exasperating and very difficult. However, you have a professional and moral obligation to meet the needs of all students. Be as considerate of these students as you are of the good citizens who earn top grades. Most school systems have special services available to assist you with these types of problems.

The purpose of this section is to make you aware that mentally ill students may be present in your classroom. You are not expected to be an expert in this area, but you must anticipate and plan for such an eventuality.

SUMMARY OF SOLUTIONS

1. Be alert for highly unusual student behavior and seek professional assistance immediately.

2. Consult with your guidance department regarding suspicious student behavior. The records may indicate the existence or non-existence of a problem.

3. Consult with former teachers.

4. Be careful not to accuse or brand someone with a psychological term. Leave this to the experts.

The Incorrigible Student

Some students seem to get involved in most, if not all, of the previously mentioned problems. These students are frequently in trouble and the normal methods of handling them does not seem to work. All too often these students blame everybody and everything for their behavior. They cannot, or will not, admit they may be partly the cause of their own problems. Normal classroom management techniques probably will have little success with incorrigible students.

If you suspect that you have a student with severe problems, consult with other successful teachers. They may have valuable advice which you can try when dealing with this type of student. If this advice doesn't help, suggest a meeting of a child study committee or a similar conference.

These teams, composed of administrators, teachers, counselors, parents, and maybe students, evaluate ideas on how to deal with the problem. This is an excellent process to establish a plan of action. Consequences of continued misbehavior must be clear to all involved, especially the student and parent.

Behavior modification has been attacked from many quarters but some educators use it successfully. An article which appeared in the January, 1977 issue of Behavior Modification, listed three rules for use in the classroom.

1. Make the rules explicit so that students understand what is expected of them for each period.

2. Ignore behaviors which do not interfere with learning, unless a student is being injured. Use punishment that seems appropriate, preferably withdrawal of some positive reinforcement.

3. Give praise and attention to behaviors that facilitate learning. Tell the student why he is being praised. Try to reinforce behaviors incompatible with those you wish to decrease. Example of how to praise: "I like the way you're working quietly." "That's the way I like to see you work." "Good job, you are doing fine." Transition period: "I see Johnny is ready to work." "I am calling on you because you raised your hand." "I wish everyone were working as hard as you." Use variety and expression. In general, give praise for achievement, pro-social behavior, and following the group's rules.

These rules seem to make a great deal of sense and could probably be used successfully by many classroom teachers.

Teachers have found that developing independent study activities around student interests diminishes behavior problems. Contracts, for both academic achievement and behavior problems, are sometimes helpful. Consider the following when implementing contracts:

1. It is written, and can be referred to at any time by the student, teacher, and parent when questions arise.

2. It is specifically stated so there is as little confusion as possible.

3. The written signature on the part of the student and parent implies commitment from both and lends an atmosphere of "legality" to the transaction.

4. Once the contract has been implemented, it may be renewed or modified on an on-going basis.

Removal from the classroom is a last resort. This, of course, requires principal approval. A final plan or contract should be agreed to, signed by student, parent, teacher and principal. When the contract is violated, immediate action must be taken. The student may be moved to an isolated room or sent home until behavior improves. Remember, this is a last resort type of action.

SUMMARY OF SOLUTIONS

1. Consult with other teachers when you have a problem student that does not respond to normal classroom management procedures.

2. Request a meeting of the child study committee.

3. Employ behavior modification techniques.

4. Implement student/teacher contracts.

5. Have the student keep a record of his misbehavior.

6. Ask the problem student to write an essay explaining how he perceives his problems.

7. Students such as these may function better on a non-traditional schedule.

8. Consult with your principal about the possibility of a less than full day schedule.

9. Discuss the possibilities of a work experience schedule with a school counselor.

10. Try temporary periods of removal from the classroom.

11. As a last resort, request permanent removal from the classroom.

ABOUT THE AUTHORS

The authors have each been involved with public education for nearly two decades. Their experiences as educators are the basis for this book.

Mr. Dittburner has experience as a classroom teacher, assistant principal and presently serves as principal of a junior high school He has always believed that classroom management must precede learning; however, it was not until he became an assistant principal that he fully appreciated the magnitude of classroom management problems. Mr. Dittburner handled the numerous discipline referrals which were made daily to the principal's office. He realized that many of these referrals could be avoided and handled with proper classroom management techniques. The years of handling referrals, visiting classes, and brainstorming with colleagues has culminated in the writing of this book.

Dr. Gervais has experiences as a classroom teacher, consultant and is presently an associate professor. As a supervisor of student teachers, Dr. Gervais has had the opportunity to observe the classroom management techniques employed by both supervising teachers and student teachers. These observations have taken place in elementary and secondary schools in a variety of geographic locations. The sum total of these experiences has convinced Dr. Gervais that there is a need for the development and improvement of skills and techniques in the area of classroom management.

These experiences have given the authors the opportunity to observe, compare and record the classroom management techniques of many teachers. The authors feel there is a need for practical methods for handling classroom problems. Hence, this book ----- WHAT DO YOU DO WHEN -- A HANDBOOK FOR CLASSROOM DISCIPLINE PROBLEMS WITH PRACTICAL AND POSITIVE SOLUTIONS.